Keeping Secrets

A Wicketkeeper's Handbook

Keeping Secrets
A Wicketkeeper's Handbook

Paul Sullivan

The Book Guild Ltd

First published in Great Britain in 2017 by
The Book Guild Ltd
9 Priory Business Park
Wistow Road, Kibworth
Leicestershire, LE8 0RX
Freephone: 0800 999 2982
www.bookguild.co.uk
Email: info@bookguild.co.uk
Twitter: @bookguild

Typeset in Sabon MT

Printed and bound in Great Britain by CPI Group (UK) Ltd, Croydon, CR0 4YY

ISBN 978 1911320 906

British Library Cataloguing in Publication Data.
A catalogue record for this book is available from the British Library.

Sunny days at Shardeloes
Safaris with Kongonis

Contents

Introduction

Sunday morning at Nairobi Club a mile above sea level. Standing back to a seamer bowling left arm over to a right-hand bat. It's the third over of the day and the pitch is helpful. The batsman shapes to play forward, defensively. I can see three quarters of the ball outside the edge of the bat so I know there's a chance of a nick coming my way. As the ball deflects off the bat, time slows down to the super slow motion of television replays. The rotation of the ball is sedate. I count the stitches on the seam and scan the gold Kookaburra logo.

I was still in the crouch position, gloves together, just starting to rise with the ball. Instantly I received a decisive, strict instruction from within. "Wait!" it said. It was as clear as a spoken command. I waited. I waited consciously and deliberately as I was: feet firmly on the ground, body moving slowly to the right, legs well bent, eyes on the ball, alert yet relaxed.

The ball was going low to my right, towards first

slip. I watched it placidly for some time. Eventually my leg muscles received the signal for lift off. It wasn't a command, more a realisation that it was time to go. I pushed off from the right leg with full thrust, yet gradually and incrementally. I felt my boots gripping the turf, thigh muscles contracting, knee straightening, the final flex of ankle and toes. The entire process of the launch was slowed and expanded. I became aware of the sequence of muscular movement and joint articulation and it felt automatic and effortless, powerful and controlled. My right arm, which led the way, stretched out as I went. From the moment of lift off I knew that my right glove would intercept the ball. I had been programmed. The command, "Wait!" had been part of the plan. My take off was timed to the millisecond and there was nothing left for me to do. I was a spectator with a great view, travelling through space with an extended right arm and a slight hangover.

I was flying. Exhilarated, I travelled through the air, eyes locked on the target. The ball was spinning slowly and it was obvious that our paths would meet. I was a space vehicle on course to rendezvous with a satellite. All the essential computations had been calculated, including satellite speed, engine burn and intercept coordinates. The results were locked-in and implemented without any conscious input. There was no suspense, no excitement, and no doubt about the end result. Docking was a done deal. It was written. It was ruthless. The batsman was already out.

Meanwhile I was cruising. My eyes remained on the ball as it came ever closer to the point of interception.

I made no special effort to catch it. My glove was always in exactly the right position and I watched the ball all the way. I don't think it would have mattered much if I had closed my eyes shortly after take off.

Ball met glove at the base of the first two fingers and thumb. They gripped the ball reflexively. A circular puff of black dust exploded slowly from the palm and drifted upward. Individual specks, like tiny grapeshot, hung in the air for a short time and fell away. Then came the noise of impact, louder than usual. I was in a world of silence and the sound came as unexpectedly as the puff of dust.

There was more. Having caught the ball, my wrist rotated clockwise so that the glove faced skywards, and then rotated back to face the bowler. This cycle was repeated. What a surprise. Why did it do that twice?

We had docked successfully but the catch was not yet over. We continued the voyage open-mouthed and ecstatic, and as gravity kicked in we slowed and started the descent for landing.

Touchdown was on a bent right elbow followed by the right shoulder, wrist, hip, thigh, knee, ankle and foot. We were still moving, sliding over grass, decelerating smoothly to a stop, my glove a yard in front of slip's right boot. His eyes were closed. As they opened, time returned to normal. I had claimed a catch that had taken perhaps one second to complete in real time, but lasted at least fifteen times as long from my perspective.

Chapter 1

How to become a wicketkeeper

"To keep wicket is indisputably the most difficult job in cricket. The demands of the job greatly exceed those of batting, bowling or fielding... A wicketkeeper must be vigilant and he must be fearless... The job, in sum, requires the concentration of a heart surgeon, the reflexes of a fighter pilot and the guts of a boxer."[1]

RAMACHANDRA GUHA, *The Picador Book of Cricket.*

The wicketkeeper, without doubt, is the single most influential member of a cricket team. During a season, no other fielder will have more chances to dismiss a batsman; no other fielder will be offered as many opportunities to be a match winner. In the field you lead by example, you are the energiser, the encourager and often the executioner. All things considered, keeping wicket is the most satisfying and rewarding job in cricket.

A good wicketkeeper sets high standards, encourages fielding excellence and lifts a team's performance when required. With the best view of the game he leads appeals for lbw and is the natural focus of the fielding side. His role is so central to the success of his team, that it is arguably the most important on the field.

Far from being merely a stopper and saver of byes, the wicketkeeper is a commando warrior whose primary job is to forge an attacking partnership with the bowler to dismiss the batsman at every opportunity. Uniquely, as wicketkeeper, you are directly involved in every delivery throughout the innings. Whenever the batsman fails to hit the ball it will end up in your gloves. When the batsman does hit the ball, the fielder should return it to you as a matter of routine to make the ball dead. During a match you touch the cricket ball more often than any other player. There is no time to daydream and zero chance of boredom. The keeper is in the frontline of battle and always in the thick of things.

Every match for a wicketkeeper is action-packed and you need to be the fittest player in your team. The mental demands of the job are equally exhausting and you will develop the skill of repeatedly switching on your concentration for short intervals during a long day in the field. This is much like the concentration needed for batting, except for the wicketkeeper there is no rest. You will never be at the non-striker's end during a maiden over. You are always facing the bowling.

There are other skills to master, including footwork that is more akin to dancing than to anything else. Don Bradman and Jack Hobbs were accomplished and enthusiastic dancers and all good batsmen dance without realising it. So it is with wicketkeepers.

Anyone can aspire to keep wicket, and any young cricketer with an urge to have a go behind the stumps should follow their instinct. Ideally you are in possession of a variety of useful genetic gifts and temperamental traits. It will help if you have above average reflexes, excellent vision, exceptional hand/eye coordination, courage, balance, agility, flexibility, a splash of competitiveness and a pinch of aggression. In addition you will need the fast twitch muscles of a sprinter combined with the stamina of a marathon runner. But above all else, the key skill for a wicketkeeper is the ability to catch.

Keeping Secret: Make every type of ball your friend.

Introduce yourself to every ball you can find, from a marble to a beach ball. Each ball possesses different properties and characteristics and you need to learn these differences to understand and master them. Include a football, a rugby ball, tennis ball, golf ball, squash ball, billiard ball, table tennis ball and any other kind of ball you come across. Always keep a ball of some sort with you. Make it your constant companion. Study its characteristics and behaviour: how it bounces, spins, reacts to various surfaces. Learn how to control it, how to catch it in either hand, how to kick it with either foot. Get to know it. Unlock its mysteries. Make it your friend.

The Welsh scrum half Gareth Edwards was an all-round athlete who won the Welsh schools' titles for the long jump, hurdles, discus and pole vault. The skills that set him apart as a rugby player were a sharp rugby brain, speed off the mark, an instinct for scoring tries, and pinpoint accuracy with the boot.

> "I must have kicked a ball since I can remember, when I was only about four. I was kicking the ball for hours on the road or in the park with friends. There wouldn't be a moment when I was not doing it. If we were gossiping on the roadside we would keep a tennis ball or football up in the air while we talked. I would kick it up as many times as I could and if it went on the ground your mate would have it. No one said we should do it but we were forever competing and what we didn't realise was that we were honing our skills."[2]

Every international wicketkeeper, as a boy, was on intimate terms with a ball as part of a regular daily routine. In his schooldays the great Australian keeper Bert Oldfield carried a tennis ball that he would constantly bounce off walls and pavements to sharpen his reflexes. As an adult, in the sports shop he owned in Sydney, he insisted that staff should throw a variety of items for sale at him to keep him alert and to keep his eye in. This dedication was taken to extremes during the cricket season when he would neither read nor go to the cinema for fear of straining his eyes.

A cricketer's relationship with the cricket ball is developed and maintained throughout his playing career and sometimes beyond. Sidney Barnes was one of the best bowlers in the history of the game. He took 6,229 wickets in his first class career at an average of 8.33 runs. In Test matches for England he took 189 wickets at an average of 16.43. The distinguished cricket writer Neville Cardus remembers meeting him in Manchester during the off-season:

> "Barnes remained a dangerous bowler long after he was obliged to give up first-class cricket. The West Indies team of 1928 played against him in a club match, and they thought he was the best they had encountered all the summer; Barnes was well beyond fifty then. His hatchet face and his hint of a physical leanness and an unsentimental mind were part and parcel of his cricket, which is perhaps best described as 'unrelenting'. In the depth of an English winter I ran into him in a Manchester street and fog. He was wearing the lightest overcoat and during a brief talk he, as though by habit and not knowing what he was doing, brought from a pocket a cricket ball and began instinctively to fondle it, twist it, roll his long sinuous fingers round it. 'Keeps me in practice,' he explained."[3]

Keeping Secret: Study other wicketkeepers as a powerful way of learning.

One of the best ways to learn any skill is through close observation. You can learn how to drive a car, kick a ball or keep wicket by careful study of an expert in action. Observation is an art in itself and it takes a certain dedication to apply the necessary single-mindedness and concentration on the subject. As a boy, the legendary Welsh fly half Barry John learned his craft by observing Carwyn James, Llanelli's fly half, at Stradey Park, home of the Scarlets. Journalist Frank Keating recorded John's creative method of learning the tricks of the trade.

> "I think for anybody learning it is crucial to watch good players in action, and watching them in a particular way. Even if it is the best player in your village, that will do. I made a point of going to Stradey as often as I could to see Carwyn himself in action. The first time, I kept my eyes on him for the first ten minutes of the match: I didn't follow the ball, I followed him, trying to keep up with his thinking and seeing what he did when he was off the ball. In the next match I covered a different ten-minute period in the same way, so that after a number of matches I knew his game very well, his defensive moves, his counterplay. When you think about it, any one player does not touch the ball much during the match; what he does when he is not in possession is at least as important as what he does when he has the ball."[4]

Barry John was studying a master fly half at work and the principle remains the same when learning to keep wicket. It is not an easy thing to do, to study a wicketkeeper exclusively, shutting out all other movements and distractions. Keith Andrew, the Northamptonshire and England wicketkeeper, was a mechanical engineer who found a way of isolating the wicketkeeper for observation. His study method, when Northants were batting, was to focus on the visiting keeper through a copy of the *Daily Telegraph* rolled up into a tube. Other newspaper titles work just as well. Among those he studied was the Kent and England wicketkeeper Godfrey Evans.

> "He was the strongest man I've ever seen. He'd been a professional boxer, and he had these terrific legs like steel springs. He could get down to the squatting position and take off to first slip without getting up, almost like a rocket being launched. I don't think I've seen any other wicketkeeper do that."[5]

The key to studying a good keeper is finding a good keeper to study. When you find one, follow him in play to the exclusion of all else. Watch him minutely, standing up and standing back. Check his position, stance, and agility. Analyse his timing and his rhythm and observe what he does right and what he does wrong. Does he get up too soon, does he snatch at the ball, is he well balanced, how is his footwork? Does he encourage his fielders? Does he offer them a target for throws? You can learn just as much from a relatively unskilled wicketkeeper as you can from an expert. In this case imagine you are his coach. Identify the mistakes in his technique and decide what he could do to improve his performance. When practising, imitate the good techniques and incorporate them into your game. If you have no access to a wicketkeeping coach, this is an excellent way to learn the habits and actions that make a good and effective wicketkeeper.

As a boy Stanley Matthews used to practise football with a tennis ball. He believed that every footballer should be two-footed and recommended kicking a tennis ball against a wall, alternating the feet each time. It is an ideal routine for a wicketkeeper. The drill is not easy. It forces precise technique, perfect balance, a delicate touch and extreme accuracy. It is tiring and requires patience and dedication, but it works. With daily persistence this practice routine will improve your timing and coordination and will establish muscle memory for the often-neglected left side of the body. In truth a one-footed footballer is only half the player he could be, and should be, yet many professional footballers even today remain one-footed. Having mastered control of a tennis ball with both feet, a full-size football is relatively easy. If you are a rugby player, especially a scrum half or fly half, this particular training routine will help you to become a two-footed half back, that rarest and most valuable of all rugby players.

The other characteristic key to the success of this training idea is its solitariness. It is concentrated, it is intense, and it is a solo effort. It does not depend on a coach, other people, or lots of props and facilities: just a wall and a ball, that's all.

Percy Cerutty was a postal worker turned athletics coach, an eccentric visionary who was years ahead of his time. He trained Australian runner Herb Elliott for six years, and for those six years Elliott remained undefeated, winning the 1,500 metres of the 1960 Rome Olympics by the largest margin in Olympic history.

Cerutty's training camp at Portsea, near Melbourne, was a wonderful environment for running. Featuring pounding surf, sandy beaches, magnificent cliffs, salty air and running tracks through the trees, Portsea offered a tough physical challenge in spiritually uplifting surroundings. Cerutty's methods soon changed the training régime of runners throughout the world. He introduced Herb Elliott to the novelty of resistance training: hill work while carrying a brick-loaded backpack and sprinting up sand dunes against the clock. Cerutty encouraged him to run barefoot; he pushed weight training as never before, preached vegetarianism, promoted a Spartan life style and a stoic attitude to pain. Above all, he offered his runners an escape from the grind of track training and a renewal of their connection with nature.

Cerutty made sure his training sessions were painfully intense, characterised by their quality rather than quantity. For Herb Elliott, wearing spikes in a race on a flat running track must have felt like a holiday in comparison to sprinting up sand dunes barefoot. The training was tougher than the racing.

Probably the best-known instance of a self-taught sportsman is Donald Bradman's highly creative daily batting tutorial that he invented in the small town of Bowral, near Sydney. At the back of his home he devised a cricket match for one player using a cricket stump, a golf ball and an 800-gallon circular water tank that sat on a curved base of bricks. He would stand about eight feet from the water tank in front of the door to the laundry. On the off side was the wall of the house, while the on side was open. The floor was concrete and the area was roofed over. Using his right hand he would throw the golf ball underarm, on the full, at the curved brick base of the water tank. The rebound was random in height, speed and direction, and the eight-year-old Bradman would cut, drive, glance or pull the ball accordingly, using the stump as a bat. A video of Bradman reconstructing this improvised training routine exists online. What is remarkable is the fact that the stump was not full-sized. It was a thin, junior-sized stump commonly used for a boys' game of beach cricket. In the online footage he never misses a ball. Hitting the middle of a golf ball consistently with the middle of a small stump is incredibly difficult, and apparently Bradman played this game day in, day out, in all weathers, month after month, year after year.

That's not all. On the evidence of the video, Bradman bowled the golf ball about once every three or four seconds. That's fifteen to twenty deliveries a minute: between 150 to 200 overs an hour. It was concentrated practice, repetitive and solitary, obsessive and compulsive; behaviour that resulted in the emergence of the greatest batsman and most prolific run-scoring machine in the history of cricket. Having proved the success of his training routine, it is faintly surprising that the Australian government fails to provide every Australian boy on his seventh birthday with an 800-gallon water tank on a curved brick base, a junior grade cricket stump and a golf ball. To discover another Bradman would be to find the Holy Grail of batting in the twenty-first century. And if the return on the investment were 0.0001% it would still be a bargain.

Bradman intuitively found a brilliantly effective way to sharpen his reflexes, to perfect his timing, to master his hand/eye coordination and to lose himself in the concentration necessary for consistency. It was the equivalent of the modern-day obsession with video games, except, while they certainly develop reflexes and brain/eye coordination, they lack the physical involvement of coordinated muscle, nerve, sinew, ligament, tendon and footwork. It is not surprising that Bradman notched his first century at the age of eleven, scoring an undefeated 115 out of a team score of 156 for Bowral High School. After endless hours of total concentration on a tiny golf ball and a stump, a cricket ball would have seemed the size of a grapefruit and his bat as wide as a railway sleeper. Bradman's daily water tank drill was much more difficult than batting in a real game of cricket.

In July 2015, Chris Froome won the Tour de France for the second time. As a teenager he had started to train obsessively in the hills of Kenya, cycling six-hour solo training rides at a consistent and uncomfortable pace from start to finish.

"The first ninety minutes would be quite bearable. After that the pain would start gnawing. My legs would put forward their case for a little freewheeling time on any slight downhill, just a small window to allow them to get a bit more sugar in the system. The brain had to win those arguments and keep the show rolling. Pushing and pushing.

By the end of the six hours the pain was a screaming presence. The last thirty minutes were the worst temptation but the best triumph. I had been doing this for five and a half hours. Maybe I could cruise home? Just take it down a notch? I had done the work and could feel the pain. Surely I had earned my parole? But my brain had to keep my body honest. The compartment that felt pleasure from suffering had to be the casting influence. Just do the last half hour. Don't surrender having done so much. Then, miraculously, when I was so near the end, my body tripped the adrenaline switch and I had the strength for one last effort. Faster, faster, and no pain any more.

I look back at it now and I can see the madness, but I like that. It was necessary. It was purging and transformative. And in terms of my fundamental attitude to training, not much has changed."[6]

The most productive cricketers are the ones who practise the most. If you want to be better than everyone else, the obvious answer is to practise more than anyone else. To succeed in mastering a skill you need to set goals for yourself and then dedicate yourself to achieving them. It is the same in any field of endeavour. Mastering a musical instrument, for example, takes the same amount of dedication. Jimi Hendrix reportedly held a guitar in his hands for eight or nine hours every day, from breakfast to bedtime, even in the bathroom. Some of his friends and colleagues never saw him without a guitar in hand. Eventually he became, by common consent, the most accomplished virtuoso of the electric guitar in the world. If you love what you do, you are bound to improve because you will practise more often. At the same time you will be relaxed and happy because repetitive, intensive, solitary training isn't hard work if you are improving skills and enjoying it.

> **Keeping Secret:** Practise the golf ball drill for rhythm, footwork and timing.

The specific, central, core skill of a wicketkeeper is catching the ball. When keeping wicket there is a rhythm, tempo and balance involved in taking the ball correctly. It is not merely a question of catching the ball every time. Taking the ball properly means correct footwork so that that the head is behind the ball on impact. A keeper's footwork consists of frequent, small, precise adjustments, like a dancer's or a tennis player's, made in response to the trajectory and movement of the ball so that the head remains in the optimum position. The keeper's hands should be held together as a single unit directly in line with the head. The eyes watch the ball right into the hands as they give on impact to cushion the force of the ball.

The golf ball drill is a valuable exercise that will help your rhythm, timing and footwork. It is a very simple and effective routine that addresses every element of catching a ball. Like Bradman's boyhood batting simulation, the golf ball drill is concentrated practice with a ball smaller than a cricket ball. In addition a golf ball has a lively bounce and forces you to react quickly and to be precise with feet and hands. It is described by Australian keeper Ian Healy as an essential part of his everyday training and also as a trouble shooting drill when he felt his rhythm or timing was fractionally out of kilter.

> "It involved finding a wall and, while wearing keeping inners, throwing catches off the wall to yourself with the golf ball [...] We never sought to throw difficult catches; the intention was not to throw it hard but to concentrate on catching the golf ball as you would correctly catch a cricket ball as a keeper in a game. We bounced the ball before the wall so it would come back to us on the full, all the while rehearsing our sideways movement, studying our catching techniques, watching the ball into the hands, practicing balance and rhythm. Then we'd move closer to the wall, to imitate keeping to the spinners [...] Because you're not throwing it too hard, you can't really get hurt with the golf ball, while getting your gloves and feet moving in all the right directions, so it's a magnificent exercise. Its other benefit is that, unlike almost every other keeping drill, you don't need someone else to help you. You can go away by yourself and work on everything you'll need, and are limited by nothing more than the extent of your imagination."[7]

Keeping Secret: Get your eye in before a cricket match – hit a squash ball.

Before the start of a cricket match, twenty minutes of practice in a squash court is the ideal preparation for a wicketkeeper. Hitting repeated forehand and backhand drives is good for footwork, timing, balance and hand/eye coordination. Then stand closer to the wall to sharpen the reflexes and as a general warm up. After chasing a small, dark ball in artificial light, a red cricket ball in daylight will seem the size of a watermelon. A squash court is ideal though not essential. Any wall will do, and it works well either with a partner or as a solo exercise.

Keeping Secret: The better the standard of cricket, the easier it is to keep wicket.

When you start to keep wicket, the pitches you play on will often be rough and ready and liable to be bumpy. The bounce of the ball will be unpredictable and you will probably be wearing team kit that may not fit. Bowlers will be erratic, batsmen untutored, fielders uninterested and their throws inaccurate. You will collect bruises because all those around you, including yourself, are unskilled. As you learn the craft and make progress through the age groups you will begin to play on better pitches, eventually on turf that has been watered, cut and rolled; where the bounce is true, where bowlers are keen and accurate and batsmen more orthodox and accomplished. Fielders will have better throws and umpires more experience; those playing cricket will be playing for the love of the game, not because they are forced to take part. Quite suddenly the art of keeping wicket becomes easier. Having learned to take all types of delivery on every sort of surface, by the time you have served your apprenticeship you should have confidence, ability and your own kit. There is no escaping your apprenticeship. The earlier you start the better you are likely to become.

Endnotes

1 *The Picador Book of Cricket*, Ramachandra Guha, Picador, London, 2006.
2 *Nobody Beats Us: The Inside Story of the 1970s Wales Rugby Team,* David Tossell, Mainstream, 2010.
3 *Close of Play*, Neville Cardus, Collins, London, 1956.
4 *The Great Number Tens*, Frank Keating, Partridge Press, London, 1993.
5 *Guess my Story: The Life and Opinions of Keith Andrew Cricketer*, Stephen Chalke, Fairfield Books, Bath, 2003.
6 *The Climb, Chris Froome*, Penguin, 2015.
7 *Hands & Heals*, Ian Healy, HarperSports, Australia 2000.

Chapter 2

Tricks of the trade

"It very seldom occurs that anybody deliberately attempts to make a wicket-keeper of a boy. He generally drifts into it quite by chance, and subsequently never receives the tuition and attention which is devoted to the art of batting and bowling, or even fielding."[1]

MAJOR R. T. STANYFORTH, The Army, Yorkshire and England wicketkeeper.

Ignore the batsman

Every ball bowled in a cricket match directly involves the bowler, the batsman and the wicketkeeper. The novice wicketkeeper will benefit immensely by firmly believing that the batsman does not exist. Convince yourself that the proper destination of each delivery is your gloves, and that the batsman is merely a necessary impediment to this end. Visualise the bowler and wicketkeeper working in partnership to move the ball from one pair of hands to another. Now make the batsman disappear.

Watch the ball

The ball is the boss. Your movements and reactions will be dictated entirely by the behaviour of the ball.

> **Keeping Secret:** You know where the ball is by looking at it. You learn what the ball is going to do by studying it.

Two essential skills of keeping wicket are the ability to sight the ball early and then to catch it. In order to catch the ball a wicketkeeper must study it for information about its line, length and speed. The earlier the information is received, the sooner it can be processed for action. It follows that the keeper should focus on the ball in the bowler's hand during his approach to the wicket. It is too late to wait until the ball has been released. The keeper's eyes must lock on to the ball in the bowler's hand with his eyes wide open to gather every bit of information about the trajectory and speed of the delivery as soon as possible.

> **Keeping Secret:** Don't simply watch the ball, count the stitches on the seam.

As the ball is bowled, interrogate it with your vision. The ball is easy to see, but it is not easy to read the maker's name or to count the stitches on the seam. When you make a habit of attempting to count the stitches on the seam you naturally begin to focus your attention on the ball earlier than before, and you will watch it all the way into the gloves. After trying to count the stitches for a short time you will discover that you are seeing the ball much better than when you were just watching it superficially. This is how to develop concentration, timing and rhythm when taking the ball. Sometimes the ball will seem to appear bigger or to be moving more slowly than normal. These are natural results of true concentration.

Keeping Secret: The next ball is the important one. If you have just fumbled a delivery or missed a chance, banish it instantly from your mind.

Your body and your mind work best when they work together. Your body is always in the present. If your mind is ahead of the present by thinking of the next ball, or dwelling in the past by thinking of the previous ball, it will not be in sync with your body. Another mistake will be likely.

Keep your mind in the present by not thinking about the next delivery or the previous one. If you understand the way your body and mind work best together, in the present, you will keep wicket well and enjoy the experience more.

Keeping Secret: Study the bowler whenever he has the ball in hand. You will unconsciously pick up body language and subtle signals that will indicate what is to come.

The bowlers in your team will have patterns of behaviour as well as movements and mannerisms of which they will often be entirely unaware. If you watch your bowlers closely, your brain will begin to identify certain actions or habits that will result in a predictable type of delivery. Sometimes, when standing up to the wicket, you will take a ball, a leg side yorker perhaps, that you "knew" was coming but would not be able to explain how you knew. This ability "to predict what is coming" is developed unconsciously and at all levels of the game. The South African all-rounder Jacques Kallis noticed this ability in his wicketkeeper, Mark Boucher:

> "He was incredibly valuable to the bowlers – and he had the most knowledgeable hands in the world. He could tell what sort of mood you were in by the way the ball landed in his hands. He'd catch a couple and then say, 'OK, what's wrong?' He could pick the away-swinger from the in-swinger before we were even in our delivery stride. He'd say, 'If I can see it, the batsmen certainly will. You've got to hide it better.' We were in awe of those eyes."[2]

True sporting geniuses work out their own methods of excellence, often in the face of orthodoxy and convention. The Australian wicketkeeper Adam

Gilchrist was just such a revolutionary cricketer and describes a particular method of watching the ball when batting.

"In truth I never watched the ball as such. Ever since junior cricket I'd practised an exercise with my vision as soon as I walked in to bat. I'd look around and find something in the distance, then focus on it. Then I'd find something smaller, or further away, and focus on that. Then another thing, and another, smaller and smaller, until I'd focused on the smallest thing I could see. So, for instance, I'd focus on a stump at the far end of the pitch. Then I'd focus on the logo on the stump. Then I'd try to read the writing on the logo. I don't know if it worked but it was my routine, to train my eyes to focus on something very tightly.

Yet when the bowler ran in I didn't try to watch the ball. If you do, it can be confusing, because some bowlers hide the ball in their other hand, some put it behind their back, some wobble it about in their action... But instead of the ball, I watched the whole 'package' that the bowler's body formed, the 'shape' he'd make as he went into his delivery stride. Somehow, when you've done it enough, you can compute all the different degrees of posture and angle for your brain to predict where the ball will go."[3]

Keeping Secret: Before the next ball, say to yourself, "It's coming to me".

Anticipation

Never think that the ball is bound to hit the bat, even the most comfortable full toss that it would seem impossible for the batsman to miss. It is the cause of many missed chances and byes. Equally, never believe that the ball is bound to hit the wicket if it misses the bat.

Each time the batsman plays the ball, imagine the ball coming through to your gloves instead, and actually go through the motion of taking it. Every time. If you get into this habit it means a ball that beats both bat and stumps will never surprise you. It's coming to you.

Keeping Secret: Concentration starts with enthusiasm for the joy of keeping wicket.

Concentration

If you are confident in your ability to catch, and your mind is without fear of injury or failure, your ability to concentrate will be improved. Concentration cannot be forced, but it can be learned. Concentration occurs naturally when the mind is interested in an activity. When this happens, the mind is drawn irresistibly towards the object of interest. It is effortless and relaxed, not tense and strained.

The more you enjoy keeping wicket the easier it is to concentrate. Jim Parks, who played forty-six Tests for England, started his career behind the stumps by occasionally playing as an emergency wicketkeeper for Sussex. He was chosen because he was such a good fielder. He found that the concentration necessary to keep wicket was exhausting.

> "A batsman has to concentrate all the time he is at the wicket receiving a ball, but he does have a respite when the other batsman is facing. Not a wicketkeeper. He has to concentrate on every ball bowled during the innings and it did not take me long to understand that I did not possess the necessary concentration. This power of concentration can only be developed after considerable experience behind the stumps. It makes a newcomer mentally tired, while the physical demands are far greater than I ever imagined."[4]

Keeping Secret: Switch off your concentration after each delivery.

To be able to concentrate for the whole of a session it is important to find a rhythm for each over. As part of that rhythm you should develop the ability to switch your concentration on and off. Wicketkeeper Paul Nixon of Leicestershire and England always did it in his own idiosyncratic way.

> "...the second the bowler starts his run-up, I 'switch on' and think only about the batsman nicking it to me. Instead of half-concentrating, instead of muttering something to first slip about something that happened last night, my whole

world must now be about the nick. If it doesn't come, I quickly analyse my foot movements, check I had been in the right place for the catch, then wrap the entire experience up and hurl it into an imaginary black bin bag. Then my mind is free to wander off, and I can talk a minute's worth of rubbish to the bloke next to me, until the bowler turns and starts running in again. Then the switch should be flicked back on."[5]

Aim deliberately to relax your concentration whenever possible: after every delivery when the ball is dead, after every return from the field, whenever a wicket falls, at each drinks break and between overs. But when the bowler starts his run-up, lock your mind into the job of watching and catching the ball. Bob Taylor of Derbyshire and England, believes that a failure of concentration is the most common cause of wicketkeeping mistakes, particularly when keeping to a spinner.

"It's more difficult to switch off with a slow bowler because there's little time to let your mind wander. But while he's walking back I look at a spot where I think the ball's going to land, and then just as he's about to bowl I'll refocus on the bowler. This helps keep my head down, and if the bowler's a medium pacer and I'm standing up to him, I'll have time to do it twice between deliveries. Nobody taught me to do this, I thought it out myself, but as a matter of interest I have noticed that the great golfer Jack Nicklaus looks at a particular spot just ahead of him before he looks up to drive off the tee, and I wonder if that's equally beneficial to him."[6]

This deliberate method of managing your concentration also works when you bat, as former England captain Michael Atherton confirms:

> "My trigger to switch on was when the bowler was halfway through his run. I would then focus intently on the ball until it was dead – a period of seven seconds, say. In between deliveries or at the end of each over, I would switch off completely, and by doing so I saved energy. This was my biggest strength as a batsman."[7]

Keeping Secret: Count the balls in an over as an aid to concentration.

When you start playing cricket you rely on the umpire to tell you when the over is finished. As an aid to concentration, learn to count each delivery mentally after the ball has gone dead, and then switch off and relax. Eventually the counting will become automatic so that you no longer count, you just know. Counting the deliveries also puts you in touch with the rhythm of the over and the tempo of the match. You will feel closer to the action and more intimately involved with the game.

Keeping Secret: Don't rise too early, because it's much easier to get up than go down.

Staying down

Especially when standing up to the wicket, staying down means keeping your gloves low until the ball has pitched, and then straightening the legs and moving the hands so that the gloves follow the bounce of the ball. For a ball wide of the stumps it is necessary to move the feet so that the body is behind the ball; but the legs should still be bent and the gloves should remain low and mirror the movement of the ball off the pitch. If the ball stays low, your gloves are already in position. If you get up too early there will be no time to bend.

Keeping Secret: Give with the hands and never point the fingers at the ball.

Glove work

When taking the ball you must give with the hands to cushion the ball's impact. It means watching the ball right into the gloves and timing the take so that hands and ball together travel several centimetres towards the body. This technique helps to minimise hand bruising, and reduces the tendency of the ball to bounce out of the gloves. In a perfectly timed take, the ball should melt into the gloves with a characteristic single muted thump. Recognise the sound and feel of the impact of a perfectly timed take and try to replicate the sound and feeling every time you catch the ball. To help your timing, practise catching a tennis ball rebounding off a wall with bare hands.

Never point the fingers at the ball. That will lead to fumbles and fractures. Point the fingers down, up, or sideways with both hands working as a unit, wrists firmly together and thumbs as open as possible. The hands should form a relaxed cup into which the ball will sink and remain.

> **Keeping Secret:** When the hands are together as a unit, allow the little finger of the right hand to overlap the little finger of the left hand.

For right-handers this arrangement confirms the right hand as the dominant hand, and it encourages the ball to squeeze naturally and easily into the right hand on completion of a regulation take. This technique is especially useful in leg side takes and stumpings when you want the ball in the right hand with the minimum of delay.

> **Keeping Secret:** Practise your stumping technique in a match at every opportunity.

Once the ball has been taken standing up to the wicket, and the hands have given on impact, cultivate the habit of bringing the ball back to the stumps in one smooth, unbroken movement, even when the batsman has played the ball. Aim to miss taking off the bails by the smallest margin possible. This habit will help you to pinpoint the location of the wicket and the action will form a muscle memory for stumping. In a real stumping opportunity your muscle memory will kick in as part of a reflex stumping movement that will be fast because it has become a reflex.

Keeping Secret: To stand up to medium pace bowling, increase the speed in stages so that you become confident and competent at gradually increasing speeds.

Courage

A keeper needs courage, especially when learning the art of standing up to a medium pace seam bowler. It is important that you first master the basic skills of catching and it is equally important to wear the proper kit, including inners, gloves, pads, helmet and box at all times. If you keep your eyes on the ball the risk of being hit is small. You must get your head in line with the ball whenever possible and your body in line behind your gloves. Try to resist flinching and turning the head away, and avoid leaving the gloves out to the side, away from your head and body. If you find the pace too much for you, or if you lack the confidence to continue, by all means stand back. It should always be the keeper's decision to stand up or back and any unwanted pressure to stand up to the wicket must be resisted.

It helps to develop a positive and aggressive attitude. Consider the wicket and the creases to be your territory, and the batsman a trespasser on your property whom you wish to dismiss. You should positively want each delivery to come to you and expect every ball to end up in your gloves. Seek every opportunity to dismiss the batsman and expect a chance with every delivery. This attitude will help to make you keen, energetic, aggressive, courageous and territorial.

Keeping Secret: Use self-diagnosis when you are keeping wicket badly.

Troubleshooting

You will know when you are not keeping wicket well because you will tend to drop the ball. Your timing will be fractionally off and you will struggle to find your usual rhythm. If you are keeping badly in a match, it is important to be able to self-diagnose the problem so that you can correct it. The key is not to panic when things start to go wrong. Instead, scroll mentally through a checklist to identify and correct the cause of the fault. There are four basic causes of poor form. You might suffer from one or more of these at the same time:

1. Lack of concentration
2. Standing up too soon
3. Snatching at the ball
4. Assuming the batsman will hit the ball

If you can identify one or more of these failings, you can address it by reminding yourself of the correct behaviour or action using the following mantras:

1. Lack of concentration – "Watch the ball"
2. Standing up too soon – "Stay down"
3. Snatching at the ball – "Relax"
4. Assuming the batsman will hit the ball – "It's coming to me"

For example, if you think you are getting up too soon, say to yourself, "Stay down!" as the bowler runs in. Or, if the problems are multiple, try various combinations of mantras as necessary. The wise wicketkeeper will not wait until he starts to make mistakes and will anticipate the possibility of a bad spell by reminding himself of the mantras for different deficiencies in advance of their occurrence.

Keeping Secret: "Watch the ball, stay down, relax, it's coming to me". It's something worth saying to yourself before every delivery.

Ian Healy took 366 catches and twenty-nine stumpings in his 119 match Test career for Australia and formed a potent partnership with leg spinner Shane Warne. This is the way Healy analysed how he maintained his focus in the field:

"Down I go into my crouch, early enough so I can succinctly study Shane's run-up and delivery, not too long or my legs will complain. I've positioned myself outside the line of the off stump so the batsman couldn't obscure my view, and now, with Shane about to come in, I go through my cues. Every ball, for every slow bowler, I'd tell myself, 'Watch the ball… move… stay down.' I've seen Shane's slow, deliberate walk-in a million times. Here's the energy through the crease… and the release. Had it been the flipper, I would have detected it two paces earlier. This, though, is the leg spinner, rolled out of the hand, not ripped… but how much will it turn? Almost immediately, I see the ball drifting down the leg side, heading for scuffed up footmarks left by Glenn McGrath's first spell. They won't affect the ball now, but later, three or four days away, Warney'll be spinning hard out of there. Now, though, I must ignore the batsman as I strive to isolate the ball. It should slide down, outside the line of the batsman's legs… I must wait for the ball, don't grab for it, eyes always on the ball, my feet taking me to the leg side, low and strong. The gloves stay relaxed to give with the ball, and in it goes cleanly. I take a deep breath, underarm the ball to short leg, and settle in for the second ball of what could be a long spell."[8]

Endnotes

1   *Wicket-Keeping*, Major R.T. Stanyforth, Gale & Polden, Aldershot, 1935.

2   *Through My Eyes*, Mark Boucher, Jonathan Ball Publishers, Kindle Edition.

3   *True Colours*, Adam Gilchrist, Macmillan, Australia, 2008.

4   *The Great Wicket-Keepers*, David Lemmon, Stanley Paul, 1984.

5   *Keeping Quiet*, Paul Nixon & Jon Colman, The History Press, 2012.

6   *Wicketkeeping*, Bob Taylor, Pelham Books, 1979.

7   *Opening Up*, Michael Atherton, Hodder & Stoughton 2002.

8   *Healy*, op cit.

Chapter 3

Standing back

"In football circles they say that a player has to have a bit of a crazy streak in him to want to keep goal, and maybe something of the sort is true about cricketers and wicket-keeping."[1]

BERT OLDFIELD, New South Wales and
Australia wicketkeeper.

The decision to stand up or back should always be the wicketkeeper's alone. While it is standard practice to stand up to spinners of all types, there is no stigma attached to standing back to bowlers of medium pace and above. The decision where to stand will depend on the bowler's pace, the characteristics of the pitch, the state of the match and the confidence of the keeper. It does no good to risk injury by standing up to bowling that is too fast to take comfortably, and an injured keeper is a big disadvantage to his team. You should stand back to medium pace bowlers if the pitch is inconsistent in bounce or behaves unpredictably in any other way, or if you believe you will improve your chances of taking a straightforward catch. The decision should not be made for reasons of bravado or ego, but governed by what is safe and what is best for the team.

A wicketkeeper should either stand right up to the stumps or right back. It is quite common in club cricket to see a part-time wicketkeeper in no-man's-land, three or four yards behind the stumps. If you ever find yourself in this territory you will do better to stand up to the wicket to take the ball at a comfortable height.

Position

When standing back, stand as far back as necessary to take the ball at about waist height, although some keepers prefer to take the ball after it has dropped a little lower, between the waist and knees. If you don't know the bowler well it is better to stand too close to start with, rather than too far away. It is better that a snick carries to you rather than falls short.

As a general guide, for a right-arm bowler bowling over the wicket to a right-hand batsman, take up a position wide of off stump that allows you to see both sets of stumps with a gap the width of the wicket in between. This is a good place to start, although your position will vary, depending on the bowler. For example, a bowler's action of left arm over the wicket to a right hand batsman will force you to stand considerably wider. The important point is to ensure a good view of the ball while it is still in the bowler's hand and after its release.

Stances

Above all, adopt a stance that is comfortable, one that gives a good view of the bowler and allows you to move instantly in any direction. The simplest stance standing back is a full crouch with feet shoulder width apart, knees fully bent, the weight forward and on the balls of the feet, the gloves just touching the ground between the feet but bearing no weight. Balance the weight of your body equally between the feet and ensure the head is still and the eyes level.

A modified position of this stance avoids a full crouch. Start with the feet shoulder width apart, feet flat on the ground, knees slightly bent, elbows resting on knees. Next, check that your head and chin are up, eyes level, leaning forward with a straight back, with elbows between the knees, gloves in front and together, weight shifting to the balls of the feet. Finally, gloves down until just above, or just touching, the grass.

Mindset when standing back

It is essential that you adopt an attacking frame of mind, confidently expecting the batsman to edge a catch and wanting him to do so. If you think of your job defensively, purely as a stopper, you will be taken by surprise when the batsman nicks a chance. You must expect a catch with every delivery, especially so at the beginning of an innings, when the ball is new, the bowler fresh, the batsman nervous and the pitch unproven. Every batsman is most vulnerable when he first arrives at the crease and this is peak time for catches to the wicketkeeper and slips.

Catches

A catch should not be missed when standing back. A wicketkeeper's catch is defined as a ball that can be reached after it hits the bat or the batsman's gloves. If you can lay a glove on the ball, it's a chance, although two hands are always safer than one. Programme your mind and body in such a way that you will make an attempt to catch every chance within your reach. Visualise your catching and diving areas on both sides of the wicket and cultivate a positive attitude in this respect. It is better to try and fail than to fail to try.

When you drop a catch, as you certainly will, forget about it. Don't dwell on it, clear your mind, concentrate on the next ball and apologise to the bowler at the end of the over.

Anticipating a catch

When the bowler bowls wide of the wicket, either to the off or leg side, the first thing to do is to get into line so that if the batsman misses the ball you are in position to take it; your head, gloves and body in line with, and behind the ball.

Cover the ground by dancing sideways low across the ground with knees bent. This allows you to rise with the ball after it has pitched. Bent knees preserve the potential energy stored in the leg muscles. Then, should the batsman edge the ball, you are ready to move your feet, or to dive if necessary, to make the catch. This is possible only if the legs are already bent. If the legs are straight there is no possibility of taking off in a dive. The best that can be achieved is to fall over sideways. Furthermore, if the legs are straight when the batsman snicks the ball there is no time to bend the knees and then dive. By then the ball will be well on its way to the boundary.

Whenever the batsman shapes to hit the ball you should be mentally and physically prepared for a catch. You must remain balanced in case the batsman gets an inside edge, in which case you may have to change direction to make the catch. An especially difficult chance is any inside or bottom edge from a cut shot outside off stump that deviates towards your left foot or wider. Only good balance, bent knees and fast reactions will result in a catch taken. And you must stay low.

Catches leg side

As soon as you see the line of the ball going down leg side, start to move. Don't wait for it, as you would when standing up.

Keeping Secret: Time your movement to leg so that your weight is on your bent left leg at the instant the bat hits the ball.

If a batsman gets a nick down the leg side, and your weight is on your bent left leg at impact, you will be able to cover a surprising distance in a dive. If the ball is missed you are already in line. For any catch standing back, anticipation is the key to ensure you are never taken by surprise, as Paul Nixon explains:

> "Some edges, when they come early in an innings, can catch you out. This one I see from the moment he swings his blade. To the untrained eye such a chance passes in a flash but as soon as bat connects with ball I know I'm going to get there. The nick has taken a touch of pace off the ball; it veers away slightly, but comes through at a decent height. I dive, arm outstretched, and it slaps into the bread-basket of my right hand – just below the creases of the knuckles, so that I can wrap my fingers over the top of the ball and hold on."[2]

Techniques of taking the ball

Most deliveries that come through to the wicketkeeper are not catches. The batsman has either played and missed, or failed to make an attempt to hit the ball. There are two quite different methods of taking the ball when standing back: the English and the Australian styles. The first priority of the English way is to move into line with the ball; to get your head, eyes, gloves, and, importantly, your body behind the line of the ball so that you have a second line of defence. There is good reason for this. In English conditions the ball often wobbles, dips or swerves after it has passed the bat and it is vital to dance your feet into the correct position behind the ball to cover any late movement. Watch the ball into the gloves every time and be prepared to adjust the hands at the last second should the ball deviate.

The Australian style is to take the ball on the outside of either hip with an exaggerated follow-through of the gloves beyond the hips reminiscent of a bullfighter caping a bull. This style may be appropriate for Australia, but it is not suitable in conditions where the ball deviates more through the air. The Australian method is less secure because the objective is not to get the body behind the ball. Nor does the Australian method encourage the lining up of the head, eyes or gloves. What's worse is the likelihood of being embarrassed by deliveries that keep on moving, with the keeper unable to adjust, resulting in byes. On top of that the style is just plain ugly and simply looks wrong.

The English technique is more consistent and effective because it is more easily repeatable. The objective is to get the body behind the ball for every delivery. You always know exactly where you have to move. The Australian method is less exact because for every delivery the keeper is trying to move just inside the ball and the desired position will be different every time and not immediately apparent. There is much greater room for error and the Australian keeper in English conditions will always be vulnerable to unpredictable deviation and will often be forced to stretch for the ball at the last second. He also lacks a second line of defence, his body.

Take your pick

Imagine being alone in a bullring, facing a fighting bull, with only a cape in your hands. Every time the bull charges, it is your job to make the bull pass as close to your body as possible without making contact with the horns. That's bull fighting. It is difficult and dangerous with no margin for error. That's the Australian wicketkeeper's way of taking the ball.

Now imagine that all you have to do is put your body directly in the way of the bull's charge so that it smashes you in the guts every time. That's the English wicketkeeper's way. It's much easier. Ask any matador.

South African wicketkeeper Mark Boucher discovered English atmospheric conditions on tour:

"Keeping wicket in England, for a youngster with no previous experience there, is a tough job. The ball tends to wobble on its way to you after it has passed the batsman – Bob Woolmer used to call it the 'corkscrew effect'. Unless you have done the job, stood behind the stumps and caught thousands of balls, it's impossible to prepare. It often doesn't even show up on TV, but, I can assure you, the ball does some strange things depending on the atmospheric conditions. It only needs to deviate by a couple of inches as it approaches your gloves to make life tricky. During one game, a delivery from Jacques [Kallis] swung incredibly late and I didn't lay a glove on it. Didn't even touch it. He burst out laughing – he'd clearly seen it before. He told me to forget about it and concentrate on catching the ones that mattered."[3]

French Lessons

When Matt Prior was selected for the England Lions against South Africa, he requested wicketkeeping coaching from Bruce French of Nottinghamshire and England at the cricket performance centre in Loughborough. Prior's first impression of French was that he was "as mad as a badger".

> "He was a bit standoffish. I'm pretty sure he was shocked that I had played so much top-level cricket while being so rubbish as a wicketkeeper… And so we had an honest discussion. It was pretty obvious that we had to start from scratch. There was some very basic work to be done… We did start from scratch. I had to learn how to catch the ball. OK I know I am a wicketkeeper and that sort of thing is rather important to my role… But I did have a problem with my catching. I was mixed up. I did not have a consistent method of catching the ball. Frenchy would throw me ten different catches and I might catch them five different ways. There is no way you can be consistent if that is the case… I needed to find a method that worked for me and groove it. I was confused. One minute I was an English-type wicketkeeper, the next I was an Australian. That's because I'd been coached by Peter Moores, an Englishman, and by Rod Marsh, an Australian."[4]

First slip placement

It is the wicketkeeper's responsibility to attempt any catch within his reach and he has licence to set the limit of his own range. When you have selected your own place to stand for a particular bowler, place your first slip where you want him. Your objective should be to avoid any misunderstanding between you and first slip, especially the sad and embarrassing spectacle of a ball being edged between you with neither attempting the catch. Setting the slip cordon correctly is a key part of routine field placement and should be managed by the keeper at every bowling change and at intervals throughout the match as necessary.

> **Keeping Secret:** Define your diving area and command it.

First slip's position is governed by where the wicketkeeper stands, particularly with fast bowling. Generally first slip stands at least a metre or a metre and a half deeper, and by a similar distance wide of the keeper. Such placement avoids collisions and allows the keeper to go for every chance within his reach. An athletic wicketkeeper can claim more territory by moving the slips wider and should never feel inhibited or constrained by a first slip that is too close. Second slip is usually in line with the wicketkeeper and a further metre or so wider than first slip and so on.

It is important to talk to your slip fielders so that you all know exactly where you stand. If the keeper is in the wrong place, so will the slips be. If you stand too far back for fast bowling, so that you routinely take the ball at knee height or lower, many edges will fall short of the slip fielders. These missed chances are wicketkeeping errors and a keeper who takes the ball waist high is more likely to set the slip cordon correctly.

Keeping Secret: Persuade your teammates to appeal the catch, not the snick.

An unexpected, early shout can cause a wicketkeeper or slip fielder to freeze or lose concentration and drop the chance. Explain the problem to your team and train your fielders to be disciplined and avoid this bad habit by making a concerted appeal only after the catch is held.

When the batsman hits the ball

Whenever the batsman hits the ball that is not a catch to the keeper or slip cordon, the wicketkeeper's first action should be to sprint to the stumps and prepare to accept the return throw from the fielder. The bowler should do the same at the bowler's end wicket so that both wickets are covered, both to inhibit and prevent quick singles, and to convert throws from fielders into run-outs. You should not amble up to the wicket. Instead, show aggression and enthusiasm and let the batsmen know by your actions and body language that you mean business; and your business is getting them out at every opportunity.

Endnotes

1   *The Rattle of the Stumps*, W.A.Oldfield, George Newnes, London, 1954.
2   Nixon, op cit.
3   Boucher, op cit.
4   *The Gloves are Off*, Matt Prior, Simon & Schuster, London, 2013.

Chapter 4

Standing Up

"… for wicket-keeping is an art and the skilful wicketkeeper is an artist. Like all artists he must suffer, for his gift is innate and not fully comprehended by many of those who watch. He is regarded with a mixture of awe and distrust because of the passion that he often displays for his work, and most of the time he is simply taken for granted because he fulfils duties that, because he so obviously loves them, others feel must be easy and natural."[1]

DAVID LEMMON, *The Great Wicket-Keepers*.

Standing up to the wicket is where a wicketkeeper is most dangerous. He is in the most influential position: attacking the batsman from behind the stumps as directly and as powerfully as the bowler is attacking from the front. Standing up is the acid test of any keeper.

Whenever the wicketkeeper stands up to the wicket, the threat of a stumping is a physical and psychological attack on the batsman. With his territory so closely menaced the batsman dares not take guard outside the crease, he cannot go walkabout with impunity, and his freedom to make attacking strokes is inhibited. Furthermore he must always keep in mind the location of his feet and the presence and proximity of the keeper. By standing up, the skilled wicketkeeper restricts the batsman physically by pinning him to the crease, and attacks him psychologically with the constant possibility of a stumping so that the batsman's concentration and performance are likely to suffer. Keith Andrew, of Northamptonshire and England, elucidates:

> "When a keeper's stood up, the batsman has an entirely different feeling at the wicket against a medium-pace bowler who can swing the ball. Any good batsman will tell you that… Then there's the effect on the bowler. Once you've restricted the batsman, you've enabled the bowler to pitch the ball further up, to a more attacking length, so it will do more in the air. And that will affect the field placings. If the batsman can't move about so much, you can set a more attacking field. Keep a man in his crease and you can attack him better. After all, what does a batsman do if he wants to put off the bowler? He goes down the wicket."[2]

Standing up to the wicket helps your team dominate the batsman. It gives fielders a morale boost to see pressure being applied by the wicketkeeper, and fielders' performances will tend to sharpen up and improve as they take their cue from you. The wicketkeeper is the focal point of the fielding side. When standing up, fielders know your exact location and precisely where to throw, and their work tends to become crisper and more confident. Standing up helps the fielding side keep on top of the tasks of containing the batsman and getting him out.

Stance and positioning

The orthodox full-crouch stance is to squat with feet shoulder-width apart or slightly wider, knees fully bent, gloves resting lightly on the ground and bearing no weight. With your weight evenly distributed on the balls of both feet, position your left foot behind middle and off stump, or slightly wider, and your right foot outside off stump. The feet should be parallel and point directly down the pitch. You should be as close to the wicket as possible, your eyes just wide of the off stump at about bail height. This position creates a stable and comfortable base for instant action. Above all, find a comfortable position that is easy to assume for long periods of play.

There are two important reasons to adopt a full crouch stance when standing up to the wicket. The first is to ensure a good view of bowler and ball. It is also the ideal starting position to rise with the ball after it bounces. The correct technique of rising with the ball after it has pitched is much easier than rising early and then having to bend again to take a ball that stays low. If a particular batsman's stance or bat movement interferes with your view of the bowler, or the ball, adjust your own stance accordingly.

> **Keeping Secret:** To take the ball wide of the stumps move sideways, parallel to the crease; never step backwards.

Off side takes

The first objective after the delivery has been sighted is to get your head in line with the ball. For a delivery aimed just outside off stump you are already in position. If the delivery is wide of off stump you will have to move your right foot across, parallel with the crease. This movement should be sufficient to bring your head in line with the ball and you should still be crouched. Your left foot might naturally follow the right to retain your balance, but if you can keep your left leg anchored it will help you to locate the stumps in the execution of a stumping. As the delivery rises from the pitch, only then should you come fully out of your crouched position as your knees straighten and your hands follow the bounce and direction of the ball.

After taking the ball with the correct amount of give, the gloves should move smoothly back towards the wicket even if the batsman is well within his ground. If the batsman has actually played the ball the routine movement of the gloves to the stumps is still a good habit to cultivate even without the ball in hand. Without removing the bails, this automatic action helps you to remember exactly where the wicket is located, ready for any stumping chance that may occur.

Leg side takes

The challenge of leg side takes occurs when the ball disappears for a fraction of a second as the batsman's body hides the sight of it. At the same time it remains your objective to move your feet so that your head is placed in line with the ball. To do so you have to be fast, brave, and sure of where you are going.

The first essential is to focus total concentration on the ball as it leaves the bowler's hand. Your view of the ball will last for less than half a second, and during this brief glimpse your brain must collect enough information to determine all your subsequent movement and timing. The second essential is to watch the ball pitch, if it does pitch, before it becomes obscured. This will give you crucial information about the pace, length and especially the line of the ball so that you will know how far across to move. The third essential is to move fast and low with hands together and widely spread, yet at the same time relaxed. Finally you re-sight the ball, rise with it and take it in your gloves.

Keeping Secret: Watch the ball as long as possible and move late, low and fast.

For leg side half volleys, yorkers and full tosses, you will not be able to see the ball pitch. You must move across before the ball hits the ground and, if possible, observe the pitch of the ball from a position just outside the batsman's legs. This is not easy and requires fast reflexes and instant action. There is no time to think. Eventually the mental calculations involved will become automatic and instinctive. Over-pitched balls will invariably bounce below knee height so it is imperative that you stay low in the crouch as you move, so that you can rise with the ball as necessary after it has pitched, if it pitches.

Before moving as late as possible, ensure that your head remains as still as it can be for as long as possible, gathering information. Staying low, move your left foot smoothly to the leg side. The right leg follows the left, and then your left leg moves wider again as necessary. These movements must be made quickly and effortlessly, like dance steps, with the feet close to the turf. Keep your head level as you move, eyes wide open, gloves low and together. Staying down for leg side deliveries can make the difference between a clean take in the middle of the gloves, and the ball hitting the ends of the fingers and dropping to the ground.

The wider the leg side delivery, the easier it is to take. The ball is re-sighted more quickly when it is wide, even though you have to go further to take it. The more difficult delivery is the one close to the batsman's legs. Major R. T. Stanyforth in his 1935 classic book on wicketkeeping is sure about which delivery is the hardest to take:

> "There is a ball, though, which arrives every now and again which has to be taken blind. Take, for instance, a half volley or, perhaps a little over, the pitch of which is obscured by legs, body or bat, which turns from the off just enough to

beat the bat and legs, missing the latter by the narrowest of margins. It comes sneaking round the legs at the last moment. A very experienced wicket-keeper can, and does, take this ball blind because he knows the pace of the ball in the air and off the wicket. He guesses accurately where it must come if it does get past bat and legs, and, above all, his hands give naturally to the ball at the moment of impact, even though this impact has not been foreseen by his eyes. Even then there is an element of luck… There is still, however, that unpleasant customer to consider which passes between the bat and the batsman's legs and misses the leg stump. It is probably the most difficult ball of all to take. In most cases it should be possible to see it pitch, but its subsequent career must be almost totally obscured by bat and legs, and the time available after it has passed these obstructions is infinitesimal… It demands a quick eye and a determination never to assume that it must hit bat, wicket or leg. Its clean taking is the mark of a high-class wicket-keeper."[3]

> **Keeping Secret:** Train yourself to stay down until the slow bowler's delivery has pitched, otherwise you will be in position too soon, too static and unable to adjust.

Timing the take

Staying down does not mean not moving, but it is almost as much a mistake to arrive in position too early, as it is to be too late. The pace of the delivery should dictate your movement and the rhythm and timing of the take, and once the wicketkeeper has started to move he should not be still again until after the ball has settled in the gloves.

Standing up to left handed batsmen

It is more common to keep to right-handed batsmen simply because there are usually more of them in any team. When standing up to a right-handed batsman you become used to taking balls on the leg side. After a few years it feels natural. Also, a leg side take to a right-handed batsman means the ball will end up in your right hand, the stronger hand if you are right handed, making it easy to whip the glove back to the wicket for a stumping.

When standing up to a left-handed batsman, a leg side take feels different. It seems less natural. You don't do it as often. The ball ends up in your weaker left hand making stumping a shade more difficult. Although your footwork is similar, it is not identical, and it requires particular practice, as does the stumping movement of the left glove, ball in hand. Practise to make your left hand the equal of your right. Dancing, coordination and timing are the keys.

Catches

When standing up, you should expect every delivery to be edged by the batsman. In other words you should be prepared mentally and physically so that a catch is never a surprise and your gloves are always in the right place.

To maximise your chance of holding an edged catch, line up the inside glove with the path of the ball. If the batsman misses, you will take the ball in your inside glove. If the batsman edges the ball you will have presented the largest catching area possible to accept the snick.

One of the hardest chances to accept standing up is the inside edge. You might be able to anticipate it and adjust the hands accordingly, but these last millisecond adjustments are largely intuitive, reflex movements of some subtlety and speed, and they rely on concentration and a focus on the ball with wide-open eyes.

When the batsman is playing back there is less time to adjust, less deviation and a little more luck involved in taking the catch. The wicketkeeper will accept more catches the more often he places his hands in the correct position to take the ball.

Glove work

The hands work best as a single catching unit. Ensure they stay that way by gently pressing the heels of the hands together. Keep your elbows close to your body so that your thumbs don't get in the way, and relax the forearms and fingers. For some keepers the key to relaxing the forearms is to consciously relax the thumbs.

Once the ball bounces higher than waist height it

is more difficult to keep the elbows in and the catching area large. It then becomes necessary to turn your hips in the direction the ball is travelling and to swivel the hands so that the fingers point sideways, never at the ball. Watch the ball all the way into the gloves every time.

Stumping

Every wicketkeeper loves a stumping and it should always be your objective whenever standing up. Each ball bowled presents a potential stumping opportunity and you should actively feel that you want to stump the batsman at every delivery rather than to wait passively until an opportunity presents itself. This permanent state of alertness of mind will aid your concentration and help to prevent any stumping opportunity from ever being a surprise. Moreover, a positive, aggressive attitude will be subtly transmitted to the batsman who will feel increasingly threatened from behind the stumps and remain shackled to the crease.

Keeping Secret: A batsman must have some part of his body or bat grounded behind the line of the batting crease. The line itself belongs to the wicketkeeper.

All the wicketkeeping skills of rhythm, timing, footwork and balance are necessary for a successful stumping off a spin bowler. It is especially important to wait for the ball, and not snatch it. Snatching at the ball is often due to over-excitement caused by the sight of a batsman wandering out of his crease. The keeper's concentration tends to be distracted by the batsman's movement and he sees the opportunity instead of watching the ball. Furthermore the keeper will often become tense, forget to give with the ball and become impatient for its arrival in his gloves. He sweeps his arms forward and snatches at the ball. A snatched ball usually means a dropped ball and a missed chance.

The remedy is to practise stumping chances with a batsman and bowler so that you become familiar with stumping chances and what they look like. Eventually you will begin to expect a stumping opportunity with every ball bowled and at the same time learn to control your focus, your movements and your emotions.

Sometimes the ball comes through so slowly that the batsman, having left his crease temporarily, is able to return before you can stump him. There is nothing to be done about this, and snatching at the ball will not help matters. Simply wait for the ball, take it correctly, then remove the bails as quickly as possible and treat it as useful practice.

Off side stumping

There are two ways to stump a right-handed batsman from a wide delivery on the off side. The first is to move the feet and head across in line as usual, take the ball in both hands, transfer the ball into the left glove and stump the batsman. This skill only comes with long hours of practice for right-handed keepers.

The second method is to keep the left leg near enough to the wicket to ensure that the stumps can be reached with both hands, to step across with the right leg as far as is necessary, take the ball in both hands, keep the knees bent and sweep both hands to the wicket. The first method is slightly faster but more difficult to execute, and rewards the ambidextrous keeper and the keeper that practises.

> **Keeping Secret:** If your instinct tells you that a batsman is out of his ground, first remove the bails and then check the location of the batsman.

It is generally fatal to do these two things in the reverse order. If it is obvious that the batsman has remained in his ground, you should not appeal, of course. The wicketkeeper soon develops a keenly-tuned instinct for the batsman's whereabouts and is generally aware when a batsman has left his ground no matter how fleetingly. You will get to know which stroke and which type of delivery is likely to induce the batsman to leave his ground or lift his foot, or heel, or toe.

Leg side stumping

In one way, a leg side stumping is easier and faster for a right-handed keeper because it is the right arm that is the deadly weapon. You move across late, low and fast to leg, rise with the ball and take it in the usual way in both hands. As the gloves give to take the impact, you squeeze the ball into the right hand and whip it back and across to remove the bails without pause or delay.

Move to leg in a straight line, chest-on to the bowler, parallel to the crease, never stepping backwards. This method ensures the greatest reach when stumping with the right hand. The aim is to remove both bails by hitting near the top of middle stump with ball in hand. Sooner or later you will surprise yourself when you remove a single bail, the leg bail, during this process. This is not being flashy but is merely accidental, the result of not being able to reach further to remove both bails. Never try to remove only one bail deliberately. You will look and feel silly when you miss.

Keeping Secret: It is impossible to watch the ball and the batsman at the same time. It is the ball that matters.

When a batsman waltzes yards down the pitch and misses the ball completely, it is easy for a young wicketkeeper to fluff a relatively easy stumping due to a number of factors. He will become excited, or tense, or panicky, or impatient, or distracted, or all of the above. He will take his eye off the ball and fumble it, or snatch at it and drop it, or take it in front of the wicket, or knock the bails off with his pads. Experience and match practice will teach the wicketkeeper self-control, calmness under pressure, and economy and speed of movement. In stumpings and run-outs, you can save vital fractions of a second with practice, as Keith Andrew relates:

> "I trained myself to maximise the speed at which I could take the bails off after receiving the ball. The key to that was to get my weight moving towards the wicket, mainly on the inside foot. Then, as I was taking the ball, my weight was already on the foot nearer the wicket. The difference was amazing, especially with run-outs."[4]

Standing up to medium pace

A wicketkeeper who is comfortable and effective when standing up to medium pace bowlers is a significant deterrent weapon especially in short formats of the game. Standing up to a medium pace bowler is a major test of a wicketkeeper's skill. You need a certain amount of courage to start with, but above all you need confidence in your ability to catch the ball. There is no substitute for the inner confidence created by your own ability to catch.

To stand up to medium pace bowling, your objectives should be to tighten your concentration and study of the ball, to sharpen your reflexes, to move more dynamically yet still smoothly and under control. In short, to react instantly to the ball bowled instead of thinking about what to do.

The basics of keeping wicket while standing up to the stumps remain the same. The action just happens faster. Concentration on the ball is paramount because this will help your timing, footwork and body movement. Make sure your technique, when keeping to spinners, is as perfect as possible. Go through your footwork in slow motion to the off side and to leg. Rehearse your glove work, keeping the elbows in, the fingers pointing down, and the catching area large. Gradually speed up your movements while remaining smooth.

It is never a good idea to stand up to a bowler whose pace frightens you because you are likely to be hurt and will lose confidence. The way to do it is to increase the pace gradually in practice, first with just you and the bowler, then also with a batsman, until you feel comfortable standing up to that particular bowler at his normal pace. Then, when he comes on to bowl in a match, by all means stand up to the stumps. In practice keep increasing the speed by degrees and also the variety of bowlers you practise with. This way you will gradually expand the number of bowlers you feel comfortable standing up to. Stand right up to the stumps, in the same footmarks you use for the spinners. Wear all the protective gear, including pads, gloves, box and helmet. Say the mantra: "Watch the ball, stay down, relax, it's coming to me".

Trouble shooting leg side takes standing up

The cardinal sin of leg side takes while standing up to the wicket is to hang the gloves out to dry on the leg side while leaving the head behind, often with eyes averted. The head must get in line with the ball and the eyes must remain wide open. You must sight the ball to catch it. This particular sin has one or more causes.

1. Being surprised by the leg side delivery and moving too late (lack of concentration).
2. Early movement, when the legs move before the delivery has pitched, but the brain has not finished watching the ball.
3. Fear of injury.

When taking a leg side delivery there is no time to make a decision. Your actions must be reflexive and pre-programmed, honed to perfection through practice. When you see a leg side delivery you must react to the ball and respond immediately, without conscious thought. Practise leg side takes to right and left-handed batsmen and practise being decisive in your reactions so that in a match you simply flow.

Endnotes

1   Lemmon, op cit, p. 10

2   Chalke, op cit.

3   *Wicket-Keeping*, Major R. T. Stanyforth, Gale & Polden, Aldershot, 1935.

4   Chalke, op cit, p. 75.

Chapter 5

Fielding

"… the promising young wicket-keeper should be a good fielder anywhere, for then he has the basic necessities of anticipation, agility and a good pair of hands. Once he goes behind the stumps he must develop concentration, for that is the key to success and the most difficult thing to acquire."[1]

BOB TAYLOR, Derbyshire and England wicketkeeper.

The limited overs format has transformed fielding into an athletic, exciting and crucial part of the modern game, yet the skills of fielding remain relatively neglected. To many cricketers a net usually means having a bat and a bowl, while fielding is generally allowed to take care of itself. Seldom does a school or club side schedule serious fielding practice as a regular part of its training programme.

Every cricketer is a fielder. And the easiest and quickest way to improve the performance of any team is through better fielding. A side without star batsmen or demon bowlers can become dramatically more competitive by improving its fielding through regular drills and practice. Fielding consists of a series of skills that all players can improve, given the necessary commitment and hard work. In a limited overs match a good fielding side can save thirty or more runs. You can motivate fielders by setting them a goal of saving five runs apiece. That will mean fifty fewer runs on the opposition total and fifty fewer runs needed for your team.

Setting the standard

In the field the wicketkeeper sets the standard for the rest of the team. He has the opportunity to be a leader by example and this is one of his most important duties. He provides the inspiration, the motivation and the energy. He is the fielding coach, cheerleader and chief whip, with a mission to improve fielding skills for an optimum team performance.

Where to place your best fielders

An analysis of television footage from eight matches (sixteen innings) of the 2011 ODI World Cup in India revealed the fielders with the most number of contacts with the ball.[2]

Wicketkeeper – 32%
Bowler – 12%
Cover – 11%
Backward point – 7%

Midwicket – 7%
Mid-off – 7%
Mid-on – 6%

Total 82%

The five infielders saving the single are the busiest. While some players are specialists in preferred positions, and occasionally the old and the lame are hidden in the slip cordon, your best fielders should be attacking infielders saving one run. In any cricket team, and in every format of the game, the wicketkeeper is by far the busiest player in the field.

Make sure your fielders understand their primary role. An infielder is either in a catching position or he is saving one run. Fielders saving one run walk in with the bowler. Fielders in close catching positions remain static. A fielder who allows a run to be scored when he is supposed to be saving one run is either too deep, has failed to walk in, or has lost concentration.

Keeping Secret: "Walking in, saving one, it's coming to you".

The wicketkeeper can sharpen the fielding from time to time by reminding the fielders, between deliveries, of their responsibilities. He might say, "Walking in" or, "Saving one" or, "It's coming to you", or he might put all three ideas into one mantra. There is no need to address a fielder by name. In fact it is more effective if you omit any name because each fielder will feel that he is being addressed individually.

A fielder in the deep should walk in with the bowler and should avoid the cardinal sin of deep fielders on the boundary by ensuring that it is impossible for the lofted ball to travel over his head and still land in the field of play.

Occasionally a fielder in the deep will have little to do for several consecutive overs and may become somewhat detached from the game, especially at school level. Sometimes this is an indication that the fielder is out of position in relation to the current bowling and may be profitably moved to a more attacking role. Between overs lobby the captain to involve the fielder more closely in the contest.

Don't forget your deep fielders. Offer positive feedback by applauding accurate returns to reinforce concentration and performance.

Setting the field

Traditionally the captain sets the field from the bowler's end in consultation with the bowler. This is the orthodox way it has been done, probably since cricket began. The wicketkeeper, at the batsman's end, will sometimes see anomalies in the field settings, for example where a fielder in the deep is placed directly in line behind an infielder. From his position at the bowler's end, the skipper is often unaware of these imperfections. To avoid such mistakes, and for a more informed perspective on field placement, encourage your captain and bowler to set the field from the batsman's end, to see the field placing from the batsman's point of view. This is something that many captains will resist yet it is a logical and sensible idea that benefits the team and incidentally may puzzle the opposition.

Whether your skipper is orthodox or radical in his field setting habits, you should always organise and manage the slip cordon and close-in fielders, especially making sure that first slip is placed so that he does not inhibit you from attempting to catch any edge in that direction.

Improving fielding skills

A post mortem analysis of any poor performance in the field will determine that the three main causes are a lack of concentration, low skill levels, and failure under pressure.

The remedy for a lack of concentration is to share with each teammate the concept of switching on his concentration when the bowler starts his run and then switching it off once the ball is dead. This skill of summoning effortless, total concentration six times an over is the most important mental prerequisite in the field. In addition, every fielder must cultivate and maintain a permanent positive attitude. Each fielder should want every ball to come to him and must positively expect every ball to come to him. It should never be a surprise when the ball is hit in his direction. In any fielding position he should visualise the shots that will cause the ball to come to him, including the possible trajectories of catches from well-timed shots and mishits too. He must want to be a great fielder and love fielding for its own sake and he should even feel a little disappointed when the batsman fails to hit the ball his way. This mindset should be accompanied by a complete understanding of his role. For example, an infielder positioned to save the single should understand why he walks in with the bowler.

- A run-out, a catch, or saving a single is easier when you are already on the move.
- It sends an attacking message to the batsman.
- It supports the bowler psychologically.
- It is the trigger that starts total concentration on the shot.
- It is the beginning of a rhythmic, dynamic routine for every delivery.

It is common to see a cricketer fumble a ground ball or drop a catch that he would normally cope with easily, but fails to do so in a tense situation during a match. The answer is to simulate the conditions of a match through repetitive, competitive drills at match pace.

To convince your team that improvement in the field is necessary and desirable, the key is first to measure the fielding performance of the team in a match or series of matches, perhaps with the help of your scorer.

Catches taken/dropped
Runs saved/conceded
Run-outs made/missed

It is a simple matter to devise competitive drills to improve specific fielding skills. For example, for run-out practice two fielders stand opposite a single stump, one at square leg, the other at point, and practise run-outs from 10m to 30m range. The winner is the first to hit the stump five times. It is important to use only one stump in the drill because in a match the fielder should also focus on, and aim at one stump only, the middle stump if visible, not the wicket as a whole. This drill sharpens the concentration and focuses the aim, and also follows the principle of making the practice more difficult than the real thing.

Keeping Secret: Ensure fielding drills are competitive, realistic and executed at match pace.

Standard practice – dot ball

In a match, each time the batsman hits the ball without a run being scored it is good cricket and standard practice for the fielder to return the ball to the wicketkeeper. This action makes the ball dead and eliminates the possibility of overthrows. As a bonus it provides the fielder with a valuable practice throw to the keeper without the immediate pressure of a possible run-out. The best teams at all levels insist on this behaviour as a matter of routine.

Standard practice – scoring shot

Every time the batsman makes a scoring shot, it is the wicketkeeper's duty to get into position close to the stumps facing the fielder retrieving the ball. In other words making sure that the wicket is between him and the ball.

Throws to the keeper

The wicketkeeper should encourage every fielder to return the ball so that it arrives in his gloves just over the top of the stumps. It is also his job to make every bad throw into a good throw by moving to take it cleanly, if possible on the full.

Keeping Secret: For returns from fielders in the deep, raise a glove straight up in the air as a target.

Whenever the ball is hit into the outfield, the keeper should position himself closely behind the stumps, keeping them between him and the ball. When the fielder is about to pick up the ball, the keeper should stand tall and raise an arm straight above his head as a target for the fielder. In instances when the fielder has run a considerable distance to cut off the ball, vital fractions of a second will be saved if he can quickly identify the location of the keeper and therefore determine the exact aim for his throw. His prompt action may lead to a run-out or a run saved. The fielder should aim at the raised glove, not at the wicketkeeper's head or body. If he then makes a perfect throw, the ball will arrive over the bails.

Keeping Secret: Encourage infielders to aim at your head, not at the stumps.

When the ball is hit to the infield, the fielder should aim the return at the wicketkeeper's head. If he does so, and makes a perfect throw, the ball will arrive over the bails. Not all fielders know or understand these aiming techniques and the wicketkeeper should not assume that they do. The subject is best addressed in drills at fielding practice, and an occasional encouraging reminder may be necessary during a match.

Run-outs

In a close run-out the saving of fractions of a second is vital. It is the umpire's job to decide which of two events occurs first: the batsman regaining his ground, or the wicketkeeper breaking the wicket correctly. It is not possible to observe two events at the same time and a qualified umpire will be trained to watch only the popping crease while at the same time listening for the sound of the wicket being broken. His verdict will depend on which event happens first in his judgement.

Keeping Secret: Break the wicket cleanly, quickly and clinically. Appeal with confidence simultaneously.

There is no advantage in appealing early in order to try to influence the umpire. The natural order of things is for the ball to be caught, the wicket to be broken and the appeal to be made. Any variation in this order will sound unnatural and might serve only to distract or confuse the umpire or hamper your own coordination.

If there is a chance of a run-out, and the throw from the fielder is obviously going to bounce before it arrives, the keeper should first get into line, and then crouch so that he rises with the ball after it has bounced. Keep calm and relaxed and ignore any shouts of excitement from your teammates. Watch the ball and resist the urge to glance at the batsman's progress. Be patient for the ball to arrive in its own good time, and don't snatch. Give with it, and remove the bails as quickly as possible. Panicking will not make the ball arrive any sooner.

When a return from a fielder looks like hitting the wicket there is a temptation to assume that it will. It is a mistake to assume so. The wicketkeeper must believe the ball will miss the wicket and prepare accordingly. Equally it is a mistake to somehow will the ball to hit the wicket. It won't.

When a batsman is running behind the wicketkeeper and out of his vision, it can be difficult to decide whether or not to remove the bails in a close race. The fielding side will usually assist with verbal advice and the keeper should always take the bails off rather than leave them on if he thinks it will be a close call. No harm is done in these instances and the action adds spice and interest to the contest. It is also useful practice for the real thing.

When a batsman taps the ball and runs, the wicketkeeper must be alert to the chance of a run-out by fielding the ball himself and throwing, usually at the non-striker's wicket. He must remove the glove from his throwing hand, gather the ball one-handed, and throw directly at the base of middle stump. By aiming at the base, the ball is sure of not passing over the top of the stumps, a waste of a good throw if it is otherwise straight. In the event that the bowler or a fielder has run to stand over the stumps at the bowler's end, the ball may be flicked to that teammate if there is enough time. Otherwise go for the direct hit, throwing as hard as is necessary to beat the batsman.

> **Keeping Secret:** In a run-out attempt, ensure the stumps are between you and the fielder.

The relatively recent fashion for standing beside the stumps or even in front of them for tight run-outs is effective only if the return throw is perfect. The keeper simply catches the ball and swings his arm backwards with ball in hand to remove the bails. But if the throw is so perfect that it would have hit the wicket directly, any interference by the wicketkeeper will only slow that process.

If the throw is wide, the keeper's position next to the wicket is compromised and he is likely to become disorientated in relation to the stumps. In this case he has very little chance of a run-out. In the orthodox position, directly behind the stumps, he has a chance to sway or move to collect a wide throw before breaking the wicket, whose location he knows accurately. Also, a stance directly behind the stumps gives the wicketkeeper a better view of the ball's trajectory and makes it easier to determine whether or not the ball will hit the wicket directly.

Byes

When it comes to preventing byes it helps to develop a goalkeeper mentality; namely that nothing will pass. The dedicated wicketkeeper should expect to keep a clean sheet and should strive to do so every match. As a general rule the body should be the second line of defence, behind the gloves, and the keeper should always take the ball in his gloves and never use his pads as a first means of stopping the ball.

Taking wickets is much more important than saving byes, and the best indicator of a wicketkeeper's performance is the number of chances he accepts in relation to the number of chances offered.

Skier

The wicketkeeper should claim any skied catch within his reach. He must call "MINE" or "KEEPER" early and loudly, repeating as necessary, keeping his eyes on the ball and allowing nothing to deflect or distract him from the attempt. If two fielders are going for a skier in the deep, and neither has called, or both have called, the keeper should nominate one fielder.

Appeals

A confident and loud appeal is convincing. A shy enquiry is not. Even though either type of appeal is equally valid, umpires are human and may be subconsciously influenced by the conviction, confidence and ebullience of your appeal. For a catch it is useful to raise the ball aloft in the glove to demonstrate the fact that at least the ball is in the glove. For a stumping or run-out your body language and enthusiasm will convey the necessary belief. There is no need to pressure the umpire, or run towards him, or to behave the way certain footballers treat the referee. It is hard enough being an umpire without all that extra pressure. Appeal only when you think the batsman is out even though your teammates go up together. A good cricketer soon learns to become philosophical and to accept the poor decisions and the good ones with equal grace.

Nets

Keeping wicket in nets with multiple bowlers and a batsman is not good practice and can be dangerous. Most nets are constructed in such a way as to allow a wicketkeeper room only to stand up to the stumps and an injury is likely when standing up to a fast bowler. Furthermore the tempo of net bowling is unusually fast and bears no resemblance to the average over during a match. The keeper is forced to take deliveries from a variety of bowlers in quick succession and he cannot settle into his own rhythm. He is forced to retrieve balls in the net and is always in a rush. A loss of confidence is the inevitable result. It is much more beneficial to structure your own wicketkeeping practice away from the nets.

Frequency of skills

Reception from fielder – 39%
Underarm throw – 30%
Regulation take – 22%

Further analysis from the 2011 World Cup tournament shows that the wicketkeeper's second most frequent action is the underarm throw either to a fielder or back to the bowler.[3] This skill should not be under-rated. It is easy for a fielding side to appear sloppy if the keeper cannot consistently lob the ball to a teammate. A wicketkeeper must be able to return the ball accurately to the bowler as he is moving back to his mark without the bowler breaking stride, and while this is a difficult skill to master, it will eventually become second nature.

Captaincy

A wicketkeeper who plays with complete concentration to the maximum of his ability has enough responsibility without the added burden of captaincy. The mental and physical demands of the position are intense. Very few players are able to keep wicket, score runs, and captain a team without suffering a loss of form in one or more disciplines, and no team can afford to risk a diminished performance behind the stumps. At every level of the game the physical demands and concentration needed by a wicketkeeper are so enervating that he needs to use every break in the game to switch off, relax, recover and re-focus. While a captain needs to be able to look at the big picture in a somewhat detached, long term and analytical fashion, the keeper is completely wrapped up in every ball bowled, physically, mentally and emotionally. He exists from one delivery to the next.

Because of his position at the heart of the game the wicketkeeper makes an ideal vice-captain or trusted adviser. He has the best possible view and is well placed to offer an opinion to the captain about the condition of the pitch, the movement of the ball, the performance and effectiveness of the bowlers and the weaknesses of the batsmen. A good skipper will consult his wicketkeeper at intervals, and while the keeper should never hesitate to convey useful information, generally it is usual to allow the captain to take the initiative in these matters.

Endnotes

1   Lemmon, op cit, p. 149.

2   MacDonald, D.C. (2015). *Performance analysis of fielding and wicket-keeping in cricket to inform strength and conditioning practice* (Doctoral thesis, Auckland University of Technology, Auckland, New Zealand).

3   Ibid.

Chapter 6

The perfect performance

"In Antigua in 1981 I didn't drop a ball all day, whether from a return or from taking the bowlers. I felt at least I had achieved it once."[1]

PAUL DOWNTON, Middlesex and England wicketkeeper.

Keeping Secret: Aim for perfection each time you keep wicket.

One of the best ways for a wicketkeeper to motivate himself throughout his career is to aim to give a perfect performance behind the stumps each time he plays.

The perfect performance for a wicketkeeper is defined as one that is error free in its entirety. That is to say you never fumble a delivery from the bowler, never drop a catch, never miss a stumping, never fluff a run-out chance, never miss your own attempted run-out throw, never let through a bye, never drop a return from a fielder, never drop the ball in any circumstance.

A catch is defined as any chance off the bat or glove that is within your reach or that you have touched. The rule is, if you can touch it you can catch it. You are the sole judge of what is, and what is not a chance. Don't fall into the trap of failing to attempt a catch and then claiming, in your own mind, that it was not within reach. That is simply a case of self-deception.

Catching every return from fielders means exactly that, even a lobbed underarm toss from gully. If you grass it, your perfect performance is over. A single bye means goodbye to perfection. When standing up to a seam bowler, that difficult leg side yorker must be taken cleanly in the gloves.

A perfect performance is surprisingly difficult to achieve at any level, even for a Test wicketkeeper. But it is an excellent self-motivator and a worthy objective in itself. The possibility of achieving it increases your determination to succeed, and stimulates you to improve every aspect of your game. It banishes carelessness and encourages you to watch the ball into the gloves. Best of all it reminds you to concentrate fully on each and every delivery, one ball at a time.

In a limited overs match, for example, take note when you make your first mistake. Don't dwell on it; just make a mental note of the over and the circumstances. Then keep going, aiming for perfection all the way to the finish. In the next match try to complete more overs perfectly before you make your first error. Gradually your performance will improve. Eventually, one day, you may complete an entire innings without a blemish. This is an extremely rare event, a personal milestone worth celebrating. Your next goal is to achieve another perfect performance in the following match. Every cricket match provides one more opportunity for perfection. How many perfect performances will you honestly claim in a lifetime behind the stumps? Paul Downton achieved it once.

Next time you play or watch a game of cricket, one way of assessing the merit of the keeper is by noting how many times he drops the ball during the day. Throughout your cricket career your best performances will probably go unnoticed, as Yorkshire and England wicketkeeper Richard Blakey discovered.

"I remember a few years back playing against Northants at Luton and they batted throughout the final day, making over 350 runs. In all that time I didn't concede a bye and I didn't miss a single ball, either from the bowlers or the fielders. Other members of the wicketkeepers' union will know I am not boasting when I say it was a perfect display. As good as it gets. The best day of my career. Yet no one… teammates, opponents, scorers, Press, supporters or, for that matter the tea ladies, said a word. Not a single 'Well played, Blakes, you've had a good 'un today'. It's a different story when I shell a couple of chances, of course. And there are times when I keep wicket like a complete pillock, take one absolutely blinding catch and find people are all over me afterwards, saying what a marvellous day I've had. It's just part of the job I suppose, and down the years the lads have started to appreciate what's involved a bit more."[2]

It is an old refrain from wicketkeepers through the ages, as Arthur Frederick Augustus Lilley, the England wicketkeeper 1896-1909, ruefully remarked:

> "Wicket-keeping, like so many other things, is only too frequently judged more by results than by merit. I have on many an occasion kept wicket in a manner that has been quite satisfactory to myself and, not to be too modest, have been quite pleased with my day's work. But, unaccompanied as it has been with the dismissal of any of my opponents, it has quite failed to attract attention. But there can have been no opportunities if the batsmen have offered no chance; the bowling has not beaten the bat sufficiently. But when the bowling has been of a character to provide chances which the wicketkeeper has been able to accept, his work is more generally appreciated, though not necessarily better."[3]

It is a simple truth that most cricketers, even those of Test standard, fail to completely understand the complexities and skills of keeping wicket. Selectors, commentators and cricket correspondents are no different. Frequently, on a radio or television commentary, you will hear a wicketkeeper praised for a great catch taken when standing up to the wicket as if he had reacted to the chance. In fact the skill of the keeper is to place his hands in the optimum position to accept the edged ball. If the batsman snicks it there is no time to react, either your hands are in position or they are not. The keeper has not taken a great catch. He has merely displayed the basic skills by placing his gloves in the correct position to take the ball. The snick is incidental. He may be applauded for good wicketkeeping skills but not for making a great catch. It is quite an important point about what is possible, and what is not possible, when standing up to the wicket.

Endnotes

1   Lemmon, op cit, p. 34
2   *Taking it from Behind*, Richard Blakey, Mainstream, Edinburgh, 1999, pp. 43-44
3   Lemmon, op. cit., p. 34

Chapter 7

Kit

"Godfrey Evans jettisoned the large wicketkeepers' pads in favour of batsmen's pads in order to gain mobility and said he would have kept wicket without pads, except that people would have thought he was showing off."[1]

ALAN KNOTT, Kent and England wicketkeeper.

At the beginning of a season, in the days before Velcro and helmets, it was common for the new school or club wicketkeeper to be shown the ancient team kit bag and invited to help himself. In the depths of the broken-handled leather bag he would find a collection of fossilised artefacts: three cotton inners of different sizes with holes in the ends of the fingers; one solitary chamois leather inner, wrinkled and split, crunchy and sharp to the touch; two pairs of battered wicketkeeping gloves, the pimpled rubber facing completely smooth, or tacky and glutinous, or missing altogether; the fingerstalls like floppy, dead puppets and the little rubber sponges at their tips petrified or missing. Next, a selection of dirty, grey pads would be impossible to match for size, style or colour, all missing buckles or straps or both. Others were limp with old age or split, the padding extruding grey-black woolly stuff. At the very bottom of the bag, underneath several yellowing, flattened jockstraps, lay a mysterious web of spidery elastic joined to leather straps and rusting buckles; an apparatus that suggested a surgical appliance or an instrument of torture. Nestling in this contraption was a rusty metal box with a large dent in the middle.

Keeping Secret: Acquire your own kit as soon as possible. Get the best you can afford and aim for comfort above all else.

When you are obliged to use school or club kit, pick out the most comfortable and try to use the same gear every time so that you become familiar with it and more efficient as a result. If you are lucky and find pads or gloves that fit, and are comfortable to wear, take them home and look after them and bring them to every match.

Kit that is ill-fitting or poor quality will certainly drain your concentration and affect your performance. You will not be at your best should you become distracted by a cap that is too loose and flops about, or a rubbing, chafing pad, or boots that make their presence felt. The key characteristic of all your personal equipment should be comfort. Ideally you should not be aware of any item on your body, allowing you to concentrate fully on the ball.

Boots & socks

Comfortable boots are the first essential. Before trying on boots, ensure you are wearing a pair of thick, long, woollen cricket socks and don't hurry the selection process. After several hours squatting on the balls of your feet you can feel the position of every stud. Bob Taylor preferred to wear soft tennis shoes except on a damp day.

Shirt

Wear a long-sleeved cricket shirt that's a size too big so you won't feel tight under the arms. Button the sleeves or roll them to just above the gloves. A long-sleeved shirt protects the elbows from grass burns and therefore gives you confidence when diving. Matt Prior is convinced that a long-sleeved shirt looks more professional:

> "When I keep wicket, it is always a long-sleeved shirt that I wear, however hot the conditions. Sorry, but I think it just looks 'village' to wear a short-sleeved shirt when keeping. You just can't do that. Please don't do that if there are any young wicketkeepers reading."[2]

Sweater

Never wear a long-sleeved sweater – they are too bulky

and restricting for a keeper. Instead wear two short-sleeved sweaters as necessary if it's very cold or windy.

Keeping Secret: For support and confidence wear compression shorts or Lycra swimming trunks.

Lycra trunks

This is a fantastic foundation garment, ideal for a wicketkeeper. In the squat it gives support to groin, hamstrings and core body muscles, and its hugging quality is a real confidence builder for a young keeper. It also eliminates pinching and chafing and allows the jockstrap and box to sit more comfortably.

Jockstrap and Box

Never keep wicket without a box; the easiest way to wear one is tucked in the pouch of a jockstrap worn over Lycra trunks. Comfort is key.

Trousers

Make sure trousers are long in the leg so they are covered by the lowest pad strap but tight and narrow around the seat to support thighs and hamstrings. You may need to reinforce the back seam with extra stitching.

Inners

Cotton or chamois inner gloves provide added protection for the hands and fingers and also help the hands fit better in the gloves so that they become one unit. Inners should fit the fingers and hands snugly and it is important to choose inners before choosing gloves and to wear your inners when trying on gloves.

Some keepers wear thin cotton inners, though most prefer inners made from chamois leather or a mixture of chamois and cotton; others like two pairs for extra comfort, retained by sweatbands or plain rubber bands. Chamois inners with a towelling wristband are useful when you rip off your glove for a run out attempt. Before a match, many keepers dampen their inners by flicking water on to them, but soaking makes them soapy and slippery. A plastic bag will retain their moisture from match to match and will keep them together in one place in your kit bag. Alan Knott preferred two pairs of plain chamois leather inners: first a man's pair and then a large man's pair on top. Between the two pairs of inners he placed a piece of plasticine at the base of the third and middle fingers where he needed most protection. Experiment with different combinations and alternatives and choose whatever suits you best.

Gloves

The most important bits of kit are your gloves. Buy the best you can afford that fit your hands properly. Try different gloves while wearing your chosen set of inners and choose the pair of gloves that feels the best fit. Ensure that each fingerstall is long enough for each finger. There should be no spare room beyond your fingertips and your fingers should not feel squeezed. When you move your gloves from side to side you should not be able to feel your hands separately, or loosely, within them. Hands and gloves should feel as one. When your arms hang by your sides the gloves should not slip down. Make sure the fingertips are reinforced, the palm is adequately padded and the angle of the thumb feels natural. The inner wrists must also be protected without too much bulk. Your aim should be to find a balance between adequate protection and sufficient feel, in a pair of gloves that fit properly and are comfortable to wear. Between matches store gloves with a cricket ball in each palm so they remember what a ball feels like. Gloves that you like become old friends and are difficult to discard, as Jack Russell relates:

"I used the same pair from 1985 until 1995, using them in every game until they just fell apart. At least four of the fingers and one thumb had fallen off at various times, and had to be restitched by me. I have a sandwich box, containing needles, thread, sticky tape, black dye and other things that'll help me patch up my gear for as long as possible. After a time, though, the old gloves just weren't working with me, they were working against me, so they had to go, in case they hampered my efforts at taking the ball. So I went to South Africa with a new pair of gloves, and broke the world record with them. For once acting ruthlessly to discard old gear paid off for me."[3]

If your new gloves feel a bit stiff, don't hesitate to lay them on the grass, palms up, and bash them gently with the toe of a bat. When you wear them your fingers should feel supple and flexible enough to play the piano.

Pads

Pads should never be used deliberately to stop the ball instead of your gloves. They are primarily a confidence builder so that you can move into the correct position to catch the ball without the worry of getting hurt. When choosing a pair of pads, the principle is – the lighter the better. Ensure the knees and ankles are well protected and choose a flexible pad that clings to your leg. This is more comfortable, protects the sides of your legs and won't interfere with the hands.

Cap

A cap or hat helps to cut glare, especially when catching a skier or taking a return when facing the sun. Also, some form of headgear looks and feels the part.

Jack Russell's obsessive care of his kit extended even to his sun hat:

> "My hat has been worn in every first-class game, apart from my debut against Sri Lanka in 1981. There's hardly any of the original left, but I stitch bits on it all the time, using old cricket trousers. It's washed twice a season, and to dry it, I use a glass biscuit jar, a tea cosy and a tea towel. The hat fits on top of all three, and is then, after starching, placed

in the airing cupboard, thereby keeping its shape. I almost lost it for good during the 1994 tour to West Indies. I was sharing with Graeme Hick, and after putting the hat into a small oven, because it would dry quicker after starching, I clean forgot about it. 'Hicky' spotted the smoke coming out of the kitchen, shouted to me and I dived in to retrieve it, frantically beating it to put out the fire. I was almost in tears, what would I do? I know, I'd fly Aileen out with her sewing machine to patch it up. Hicky fell apart in hysterics and once the rest of the lads found out about it I was unmercifully hammered."[4]

Helmet

Wear a helmet with a grill standing up to the wicket, especially when keeping to medium pace bowlers. Special wicketkeepers' helmets are available with a raised back for greater freedom of head movement in the squat and a shorter peak for improved all round vision.

Endnotes

1   *Alan Knott on Wicket-Keeping*, Stanley Paul, London, 1977, p. 26.

2   Prior, op cit, p. 13.

3   *Jack Russell Unleashed*, Jack Russell, Collins Willow, London, 1997, p. 207.

4   Ibid, p. 206.

Chapter 8

The Spirit of Wicketkeeping

"When Justin Langer finds his off stump akimbo he leaves the crease only after asking the Met office whether any earthquakes have been recorded in the region."[1]

PETER ROEBUCK, Somerset and MCC.

According to the traditional code of cricket, when a batsman is given out he is expected to leave the crease promptly without showing reluctance or emotion even if he disagrees with the verdict. On occasion he is even expected to own up to something the umpire may not have seen or heard. In English county cricket, until relatively recently, whenever a batsman edged the ball to the wicketkeeper he was expected to 'walk' without waiting for the umpire's decision.

A batsman almost always knows when he has hit the ball. His hands on the bat register the merest feather touch, even the slightest contact that produces no apparent sound and no perceptible deviation. Doubt becomes part of the equation only when there are multiple simultaneous impacts: bat on pad, bat on ground, bat on boot, ball on pad, ball on body, ball on clothing or any combination thereof. In these instances, whenever there is any doubt in the batsman's mind, he is entitled to wait for the umpire to give his decision. Indeed it is the sensible, prudent and logical thing to do. But even in the case of multiple impacts, a batsman often knows when one of them is bat on ball.

The convention of 'walking' is by no means universal. In the north of England, players in league clubs prefer to wait for the umpire's decision and Australia is a nation of non-walkers with a few notable exceptions. This was one of the cultural differences that caused friction between the two cricketing nations; friction that today has escalated into an arms race between England, the amateurs who walked, and Australia, the professionals who did not.

This conflict, calculated to keep opposition teams off balance and at a disadvantage, was instigated by Australia. Other countries were forced to adopt the same measures or perish. When England visited Australia in 1982-83 the English team made a collective decision not to walk, the logic being that the Australians never did, so why should they. The problem is that Australians truly believe they are not cheating by not walking. They believe it is the umpire's job to give the batsman out and because nobody walks these days, not walking has become the behavioural standard and therefore, they feel, it is acceptable. The English, until recently, believed they were cheating when they did not walk, but in Ashes Test matches they felt obliged to not walk to keep 'a level playing field' with the Australians. Jim Parks, the Sussex and England wicketkeeper, was convinced the Australians started the practice of not walking on the Ashes tour of 1965/66.

> "Bill Lawry was a dour, gritty opener who believed that decisions of fact on a cricket field are solely the umpire's responsibility with which it would be impertinent to interfere. Along with other overseas players, notably the South Africans, Lawry regarded 'walking', which had always been the custom in county cricket, as a quaint English tradition… [In the first Test, at Brisbane] Brown opened the bowling and on the seventh ball of his first over 'I caught Lawry off his glove down the leg-side. I appealed but it was turned down. Lawry was the first of the non-walkers'."[2] [Lawry went on to score 166.]

In their attitude to the game the Australians were more mentally and physically robust than the English. They played rougher and tougher and gruffer, and would always seek to gain an advantage, both on and off the field. Traditionally, after a day's play, both teams would have a drink together, but in the 1980s Australia captain Allan Border put a stop to that practice. A ban on fraternising with the enemy kept the atmosphere edgy, and the age-old social custom of sharing a beer with the opposition was needlessly lost. Australia publicly adopted a 'win at all costs' approach to the game, as expressed by Mark Waugh where batsmen who walked would not be welcome in the Australian team. The most recent escalation in the arms race is a preconceived form of sledging tailored to individual players who are subjected to personal, scripted, customised abuse.

In the 1960s, according to Mike Brearley, non-walkers were considered cheats. The Gloucestershire seamer Brian Brain confirmed as much in his disarmingly frank diary, *Another Day, Another Match*.[3]

> "When I started in county cricket [in 1959], the ones who didn't walk could be counted on the fingers of one hand and they'd be given a huge rocket from their captain if they stood their ground when they knew they were out... [In 1980] I didn't see one batsman walk."[4]

The transition from a majority of walkers to a majority of non-walkers in county cricket was complete in a couple of decades. There was much debate, soul searching and indecision along the way. England wicketkeeper Alan Knott reflected the confusion felt by players in response to internal and external pressures by deciding to become a selective walker: "In county cricket I walk, in Test cricket I don't."[5]

Others accepted the inevitability of following the lead of the Australians. A typical viewpoint was the Australian captain Allan Border's conviction that just as the batsmen and bowlers have a job to do, the umpires have a specific job of making decisions, and it is best to leave it to them.[6]

Almost immediately after they stopped walking, English county players started to feel vaguely guilty and began to express nostalgia for the lost days of innocence and integrity and the habit of a lifetime.

"There was a time when a batsman automatically set off back to the pavilion if it was obvious he had touched the ball on its way through to the keeper. And I was definitely a member of the walking fraternity... Nowadays, though, nobody walks, ever. I've seen batsmen caught at second slip who have stood their ground and waited for the finger to be raised. Now that really is going a bit far. But with caught-behind appeals, we let the umpire make the decision. And if he gets it wrong, so be it."[7]

In the first Ashes Test at Trent Bridge in 2013, Stuart Broad refused to walk after he edged a ball to first slip via the wicketkeeper's gloves and was given not out. In many respects the incident was reminiscent of Diego Maradona's "hand of God" goal for Argentina against England in the World Cup of 1986. The similarity being that the whole world saw the incident for what it was, except the one person who mattered. In Maradona's case it was the referee. In Broad's case it was the umpire. Most spectators, cricket lovers and commentators thought Broad should have walked.

Martin Samuel, writing for the *Daily Mail*, pulled no punches:

"Of course he should have walked. Turned on his heel and headed back to the pavilion, not a backward glance, not a second thought. The professionals, sad to say, are almost universally in denial on this. It does not make a man a fiercer competitor if he plays to the bitter letter of the law. It is not always up to the umpire to make the call. There is such a thing as basic, common decency. Being a good sport, being a straight up guy. Golfers, snooker players call penalties on themselves. Why not cricketers? There's absolutely no difference between a batsman nicking it and refusing to walk, and a footballer diving to win a penalty. It's cheating, plain and simple."[8]

Not walking now seemed to be an official England team policy. England's coach Andy Flower echoed the entrenched Australian view by giving his unequivocal backing to the batsman's decision not to walk:

"Stuart Broad, like every other batsman in international cricket, has the right to wait for the umpire to make his decision. The umpire's job is to make those decisions."[9]

More wittily, Sir Ian Botham in the *Daily Mirror* wondered what all the fuss was about.

"He's got away with one. Good luck to him. If you're going to start banning [walking] and taking action against players who don't walk, then Australia wouldn't have a cricket team."[10]

The growing tendency to await the umpire's decision instead of walking put more burden on the umpire, and the introduction of technology for televised matches raised the pressure still further. In the Stuart Broad incident the Australians had no TV reviews remaining and thus were not able to arrive at a just conclusion.

The annual Spirit of Cricket Cowdrey Lecture was started in 2001 in memory of Lord Cowdrey of Tonbridge. In his 2007 lecture, Christopher Martin-

Jenkins, a cricket commentator, journalist and past-president of MCC addressed the subject of walking.

> "The life of the umpires at every level of the game would be immeasurably easier, if it were to become once more the inviolable custom of every cricketer to walk to the pavilion the moment he knows beyond doubt that he is out.
>
> That is the way I was taught to play cricket. I believe it to be in the true spirit of the game, and that what one might call the Southern Hemisphere view – that the umpire is there to decide if the batsman is out or not – is rubbish and has been responsible for a demeaning of that spirit. I give you simple evidence. When a batsman is bowled, he walks; when a batsman hits the ball in the air to mid-off and is caught, he walks. When a batsman snicks Monty Panesar to slip via the wicketkeeper's glove and is caught by slip, he walks. But when a batsman snicks it into the keeper's gloves only – and not into the fielder's hands – he doesn't walk, in the hope that the umpire might not be certain. Where is the logic, or the honour in that?
>
> Umpires need the help of players because there can be no organised game without umpires. Walking helps them. It used to be the convention in England... and should be again, here and everywhere, because it is the honest and decent thing to do. Not walking when you know you are out is dishonest... Cricket would instantly become a better game if young cricketers in every country were to be taught from now onwards that walking is the right thing to do when they know they are genuinely out."[11]

The definition of what constituted cheating in cricket was beginning to be examined more and more closely. Martin Williamson of ESPN Cricinfo is of the opinion that not walking is not cheating. On the other hand he believes that claiming a catch you know you have not caught cleanly is cheating. So is claiming a bat-pad catch when you know it was nowhere near the edge. The difference, he asserts, is that in one you are leaving the umpire to make the decision, in the other you are openly trying to *deceive* him.[12]

Williamson doesn't seem to understand that when a batsman knows he has hit the ball and leaves the umpire to make the decision, he is again openly trying to deceive him. The batsman knows the fact of the matter, just as the fielder knows in the other two instances cited. In all three cases the player knows the truth and there is no difference between them. Not walking is cheating.

Michael Parkinson, writing in *The Telegraph*, noted that some forms of cheating were becoming more acceptable than others:

"[Michel Atherton] listed the ways players could improve the current situation thus: 'I believe that dissent, abusing umpires and clear cheating, such as scooping up a catch on the half-volley, has no place in the game'. He makes no mention of batsmen not walking when they know they have hit the ball, which, some would argue, is the basest form of cheating. Atherton is not a walker. He is not the only one. But because everybody is at it doesn't make it acceptable. It simply underlines the moral confusion existing in the modern game. In defining what he describes as 'clear cheating', Atherton seems to imply that there exists a code of practice whereby some cheating may be acceptable. In other words he draws the line between a fielder claiming a catch he knows to have hit the deck and a batsman not walking when he knocks the cover off the ball. In fact, both involve skulduggery and the perpetrator is a cheat."[13]

When a batsman nicks the ball he knows what he has done and so he has more factual information than the umpire. There is a huge difference between waiting for a decision in the case of genuine doubt, and waiting for a decision when the batsman already knows there is no doubt at all. To await a decision about a fact that you already know the truth about is cynical, deceitful, disrespectful, unsportsmanlike and deliberate cheating.

If the batsman knows he is out, the only reason to loiter at the crease is in the hope and expectation of a reprieve from the umpire. That is cheating. It is also disrespectful to the umpire, the bowler, the wicketkeeper, the opposing team, the spectators and the game's traditional values. Each time a batsman does not walk he brings the game into disrepute through his cheating. The question then becomes 'Does cheating matter any more?' Are cricketers prepared to be called cheats? Is the win-at-all-costs attitude the prevailing philosophy, even to the extent of blatant cheating?

After five overs of the 2003 World Cup semi-final between Australia and Sri Lanka in Port Elizabeth, skipper Jayasuriya brought on spinner Aravinda da Silva. Adam Gilchrist had scored 22 out of 34 and was on strike. He pushed the first ball of the over to cover.

The second was more flighted and Gilchrist shaped to sweep it behind square leg. He connected with a thick bottom edge, the ball cannoned into his front pad just above the ankle and ballooned into the air to be caught by wicketkeeper Kumar Sangakkara.

"When I saw Rudi [Koertzen] shaking his head [not out] I heard an emphatic voice in mine.

'Go. Walk.'

So I walked… There were other voices in my head too, telling me I was crazy, I was defying what all cricketers did, I was throwing the World Cup away. Could I rewind the last minute? Could I go back? No. The dominant voice was like a schoolteacher, calling the others to order and reassuring me that I'd done the right thing."[14]

On his return to the Australian dressing room Gilchrist was given the silent treatment and felt more lonely than he had ever felt among a cricket team.

"Implicitly, I was made to feel selfish, as if I was walking for the sake of my own clean image, thereby making everyone else look dishonest. My action in the 2003 World Cup semi-final had become such a big deal because it held up a mirror to every player. And nobody wants to see themselves reflected when they have resisted doing what they know, deep down, is the honest thing. It was safer to stick together, to have a unified approach which rejects walking. By doing it I was breaking ranks."[15]

Over the next few weeks, months and even years, Gilchrist was applauded and vilified in equal measure. He was canonised by the English and demonised by Australians to such an extent that this particular walk came to define his entire career.

> "I was committed to walking because as a player I had the ability to make the game, in a tiny little way, better when I left it than when I found it. Umpires do make mistakes, they're only human, and I believe if batsmen walk when they know they're out, they are taking up an opportunity to reduce the number of incorrect decisions that umpires make. How is that not a good thing?"[16]

In 1989, at the age of seventeen, Gilchrist had won a scholarship to play cricket in England for Richmond in Middlesex. It was a five months spell that was to influence his development as a cricketer and a person, playing seventy-seven games against strong club opposition and learning how to make runs in English conditions. In one match, when on 93, he played a faint edge to a late cut and when the fielding side appealed, he walked. By the end of the summer he had scored eleven centuries, twelve fifties and averaged 73. He had arrived in England as a boy and returned to Australia a man.

> "I love England. I have always loved playing cricket there – the fresh green smell of the grounds, the superb facilities, the pride they take in their game, their knowledge when they talk about it. I also love the lifestyle, the sense of humour, even the food. I feel comfortable there."[17]

Gilchrist was fortunate to have had the experience of playing cricket in England where the game, at club level, is still played not only within its laws but also within the spirit of the game. The debate on whether or not a batsman should walk has raged for years in clubs, pavilions, pubs and blogs. Even the MCC weighs in online occasionally.

> "The key principles of the Spirit of Cricket is that of respect, namely for your opponents, for your own captain and team, for the umpires and for the game's traditional values. Whilst some think that a batsman not 'walking' is cheating, others feel that it is up to the umpire to make a decision. The key point is that the players must accept all the umpires' decisions in good grace, particularly if they disagree with it. There will never be a right answer to the debate. In an ideal world everyone would 'walk' if they know they have hit the ball but it is unrealistic to expect everyone to do so. In MCC's own matches, the majority of which are against schools, its batsmen are strongly encouraged to 'walk'."[18]

Those against walking say a batsman who walks after the umpire has given him not out is effectively letting everyone know the umpire is mistaken, thus robbing him of respect and authority. This is a cynical, superficial and hypocritical argument. It fails to acknowledge the fact that the batsman has more information than the umpire and it is the batsman's refusal to act on this knowledge that robs the game of dignity and the umpire of respect and authority.

The problem with walking is that, by definition, it

is both unenforceable and impossible to ban. Walking relies solely on a player's sense of honour and integrity and if a cricketer is prepared to sacrifice those virtues and cheat in order to continue his innings there is nothing much to be done. Banning batsmen from walking would be anathema to MCC and to every cricketer who is a walker, and how would a batsman be penalised if he decided to walk anyway? Tinkering with walking would simply open several more cans of worms. What are needed are administrators and selectors of character, and strong captains who openly despise the thought of cheating.

> "Looking for solutions, you begin to feel like some old buffer in a club tie counting ghosts at Lord's. Old-fashioned words spring to mind like 'chivalrous', nowadays becoming redundant because it means being courteous and honourable and therefore has no place in the lexicon of modern sport. Today's athletes would no doubt believe that being chivalrous indicates weakness, lacking 'bottle'. They should know it requires greater character to do the right thing and that cheating is the preferred choice of the weak and spineless."[19]

Keeping Secret: If your skipper, coach or teammate gives you stick for walking, stay calm, look him in the eye, smile and say, "That's how I play".

Endnotes

1   *The Bowler's Holding, the Batsman's Willey*, Geoff Tibballs, Random House, London, 2008, p. 63.

2   *Young Jim*, Derek Watts, Tempus, Gloucestershire, 2005, pp. 170/171.

3   *Another Day, Another Match*, Brian Brain, Allen & Unwin, London, 1981.

4   *ESPN Sports Media*, Rob Steen, 'Tendulkar and the wisdom of walking', March 24, 2011.

5   *"What are the Butchers for?"* Lawrence Booth, Bloomsbury, London, 2009.

6   Storify, Andrew Gilchrist, September 2014

7   Blakey, op cit, p. 52/53.

8   eNews Channel Africa, July 18, 2013

9   *The Guardian,* July 15, 2013.

10 eNews, op.cit.

11 MCC Spirit of Cowdrey Lecture, Christopher Martin-Jenkins, 2007.

12 'Not walking is not cheating', Martin Williamson, ESPN Cricinfo, January 6, 2008.

13 *The Telegraph*, Michael Parkinson, March 18, 2001.

14 Gilchrist, op cit, p. 368/9.

15 Gilchrist, Ibid, p. 579.

16 Gilchrist, Ibid, p. 577.

17 Gilchrist, Ibid, p. 43.

18 'Not "walking" = cheating(?) MCC', Planet Cricket Forum, July 13, 2013.

19 Parkinson, Ibid.

Chapter 9

Wicketkeeping and the Laws of Cricket

"I learned more in my first year as an umpire than in all the previous twenty-six years of playing the game."[1]

E. J. 'Tiger' Smith, Warwickshire and England wicketkeeper.

It is the duty of every player to know the forty-two Laws of cricket. The typical cricketer picks up knowledge of the Laws haphazardly throughout his career from players and umpires, through anecdote and by osmosis. It is far better to know the Laws as a whole rather than to learn about them piecemeal. Familiarity with the Laws will make you a more complete cricketer and give you a deeper insight to the game itself. Most importantly, your knowledge of the Laws shows respect for your fellow cricketers, for umpires and for cricket.

> **Keeping Secret:** Make sure you know the Laws of cricket so that you can appeal with confidence and debate with certainty.

It makes no sense to play cricket for several decades without knowing and understanding the Laws that govern the game. Most players feel they know the Laws fairly well, yet are often surprised by how little they really know. For example, many cannot list the ten ways a batsman may be given out on appeal. Regardless of whether you can or cannot, consider reading *Tom Smith's Cricket Umpiring and Scoring*[2], where the Laws are written in a straightforward, legalistic way to avoid ambiguity. They are explained and simplified with copious notes that make them easier to understand.

Extracts from the Laws directly affecting the wicketkeeper:

Law 23: Dead ball

1. BALL IS DEAD
(a) The ball becomes dead when
    (i) it is finally settled in the hands of the wicketkeeper or the bowler.

2. BALL FINALLY SETTLED
    Whether the ball is finally settled or not is a matter for the umpire alone to decide.

5. BALL CEASES TO BE DEAD
    The ball ceases to be dead – that is, it comes into play – when the bowler starts his run up or, if he has no run up, his bowling action.

Law 25: Wide ball

8. OUT FROM A WIDE
    When Wide ball has been called, neither batsman shall be out under any of the Laws except 33 (Handled the ball), 35 (Hit wicket), 37 (Obstructing the field), 38 (Run out) or 39 (Stumped).
    [NB You can stump a batsman very satisfyingly from a wide.]

Law 28: The wicket is put down

1. WICKET PUT DOWN
(a) The wicket is put down if a bail is completely removed from the top of the stumps, or a stump is struck out of the ground,
    (i) by the ball, or
    (v) by a fielder with his hand or arm, providing that the ball is held in the hand or hands so used, or in the hand of the arm so used. The wicket is also put down if a fielder strikes or pulls a stump out of the ground in the same manner.

Law 29: Batsman out of his ground

1. WHEN OUT OF HIS GROUND
(a) A batsman shall be considered to be out of his ground unless his bat or some part of his person is grounded behind the popping crease at that end.
    [The term popping crease refers to the early history of cricket, when a batsman used to have to 'pop'

his bat into a small hole that was located in the middle of the crease for a run to count. For a player to run a batsman out, he had to pop the ball into the hole before the bat was grounded in it. Source: Wikipedia.]

Law 32: Caught

3. A FAIR CATCH
   A catch shall be considered to have been fairly made if
(b) the ball is hugged to the body of the catcher or accidentally lodges in his clothing or, in the case of the wicketkeeper only, in his pads. However it is not a fair catch if the ball lodges in a protective helmet worn by a fielder. See Law 23 (Dead ball).

Law 39: Stumped

1. OUT STUMPED
(a) The striker is out Stumped, except as in 3 below, if
   (i) a ball which is not a No ball is delivered and
   (ii) he is out of his ground, other than as in 3 (a) below and
   (iii) he has not attempted a run when (iv) his wicket is fairly put down by the wicketkeeper without the intervention of another fielder.
   Note, however, Laws 2.8(c) (Transgression of the Laws by a batsman who has a runner) and 40.3 (Position of the wicketkeeper).
(b) The striker is out Stumped if all the conditions of

(a) above are satisfied, even though a decision of Run out would be justified.

2. BALL REBOUNDING FROM WICKETKEEPER'S PERSON

(a) If the wicket is put down by the ball, it shall be regarded as having been put down by the wicketkeeper if the ball

(i) rebounds on to the stumps from any part of the wicketkeeper's person or equipment other than a protective helmet, or

(ii) has been kicked or thrown on to the stumps by the wicketkeeper.

(b) If the ball touches a protective helmet worn by the wicketkeeper, the ball is still in play but the striker shall not be out Stumped. He will, however, be liable to be Run out in these circumstances if there is subsequent contact between the ball and any fielder. Note, however, 3 below.

3. NOT OUT STUMPED

(a) Notwithstanding 1 above, the striker will not be out Stumped if he has left his ground to avoid injury, when his wicket is put down.

(b) If the striker is not out Stumped he may, except in the circumstances of Law 38.2 (e), be out Run out if the conditions of Law 38 (Run out) apply.

Law 40: The wicketkeeper

1. PROTECTIVE EQUIPMENT

The wicketkeeper is the only fielder permitted to wear gloves and external leg guards. If he does so these are to be regarded as part of his person for the purposes of Law 41.2 (Fielding the ball). If by his actions and positioning it is apparent to the umpires that he will not be able to discharge his duties as a wicketkeeper, he shall forfeit this right and also the right to be recognised as a wicketkeeper for the purposes of Laws 32.3 (A fair catch), 39 (Stumped), 41.1 (Protective equipment), 41.5 (Limitation of on-side fielders) and 41.6 (Fielders not to encroach on pitch).

2. GLOVES

If, as permitted under 1 above, the wicketkeeper wears gloves, they shall have no webbing between the fingers except joining index finger and thumb, where webbing may be inserted as a means of support. If used, the webbing shall be

(a) a single piece of non-stretch material which, although it may have facing material attached, shall have no reinforcements or tucks.

(b) such that the top edge of the webbing

(i) does not protrude beyond the straight line joining the top of the index finger to the top of the thumb.

(ii) is taut when a hand wearing the glove has the thumb fully extended.

3. POSITION OF THE WICKETKEEPER

The wicketkeeper shall remain wholly behind the

wicket at the striker's end from the moment the ball comes into play until

(a) a ball delivered by the bowler

either (i) touches the bat or person of the striker,

or (ii) passes the wicket at the striker's end,

or (b) the striker attempts a run.

In the event of the wicketkeeper contravening this Law, the striker's end umpire shall call and signal No ball as soon as possible after the delivery of the ball.

[NB The wicketkeeper may not have any part of his person or kit further forward than the back of the stumps from the moment the bowler starts his run up.]

4. MOVEMENT BY WICKETKEEPER

It is unfair if the wicketkeeper standing back makes a significant movement towards the wicket after the ball comes into play and before it reaches the striker. In the event of such unfair movement by the wicketkeeper, either umpire shall call and signal Dead ball. It will not be considered a significant movement if the wicketkeeper moves forward a few paces for a slower delivery.

5. RESTRICTIONS   ON   ACTION   OF WICKETKEEPER

If, in the opinion of either umpire, the wicketkeeper interferes with the striker's right to play the ball and to guard his wicket, Law 23.4(b)(vi) (Umpire calling and signalling Dead ball) shall apply.

If, however, either umpire considers that the interference by the wicketkeeper was wilful, then Law 42.4 (Deliberate attempt to distract striker) shall also apply.

6. INTERFERENCE WITH WICKETKEEPER BY STRIKER

If, in playing at the ball, or in the legitimate defence of his wicket, the striker interferes with the wicketkeeper, he shall not be out except as provided for in Law 37.3 (Obstructing a ball from being caught).

> **Keeping Secret:** Volunteer to stand as umpire at every opportunity.

Endnotes

1 *'Tiger' Smith of Warwickshire and England*, Patrick Murphy, Lutterworth Press, Guildford, 1981, p. 74.

2 *Tom Smith's Cricket Umpiring and Scoring*, Weidenfeld & Nicolson, London, 2011.

Chapter 10

A summary of Secrets

"Do your best at each and every thing. That is the key to success. Learn one thing well and you will learn to understand ten thousand things."[1]

AWA KENZO, *Zen Bow, Zen Arrow*.

1 How to become a wicketkeeper

- Make every type of ball your friend.
- Study other keepers as a powerful way of learning.
- Make sure your training is harder than the game itself.
- Practise the golf ball drill for rhythm, footwork and timing.
- Get your eye in before a match – hit a squash ball.
- The better the standard of cricket, the easier it is to keep wicket.

2 Tricks of the trade

- You know where the ball is by looking at it. You

learn what the ball is going to do by studying it.

- Don't simply watch the ball, count the stitches on the seam.
- The next ball is the important one. If you fumble a delivery or miss a chance, banish it instantly from your mind.
- Study the bowler with the ball in hand. You will unconsciously pick up body language and subtle signals that will indicate what is to come.
- Before each ball, say to yourself, "It's coming to me".
- Concentration starts with enthusiasm for the joy of keeping wicket.
- Switch off your concentration after each delivery.
- Count the balls in an over as an aid to concentration.
- Don't rise too early, because it's much easier to get up than go down.
- Give with the hands and never point the fingers at the ball.
- Keep the hands together as a unit and allow the little finger of the right hand to overlap the little finger of the left hand.
- Practise your stumping technique in a match at every opportunity.
- To stand up to medium pace bowling, increase the speed in stages so that you become confident and competent at gradually increasing speeds.
- Use self-diagnosis when you are keeping wicket badly.
- "Watch the ball, stay down, relax, it's coming to me". A mantra for every delivery.

3   Standing back

- Choreograph your movement to the leg side so that your weight is on your bent left leg at the instant the bat hits the ball.
- Define your diving area and command it.
- Persuade your teammates to appeal the catch and not the snick.

4   Standing up

- When taking the ball wide of the stumps move sideways, parallel to the crease, never step backwards.
- For leg side takes watch the ball as long as possible and move late, low and fast.
- Train yourself to stay down until the slow bowler's delivery has pitched, otherwise you will be in position too soon, too static and unable to adjust.
- A batsman must have some part of his body or bat grounded behind the line of the batting crease. The line itself belongs to the wicketkeeper.
- If your instinct tells you that the batsman is out of his ground, first remove the bails and then check the location of the batsman.
- It is impossible to watch the ball and the batsman at the same time. It is the ball that matters.

5   Fielding

- Ensure fielding drills are competitive, realistic and executed at match pace.

- For returns from fielders in the deep, raise a glove straight up in the air as a target.
- Encourage infielders to aim at your head, not at the stumps.
- Break the wicket cleanly, quickly and clinically. Appeal confidently simultaneously.
- In a run out attempt, ensure the stumps are between you and the fielder.
- Remind fielders by saying "Walking in, saving one, it's coming to you".

6   **The Perfect Performance**

- Aim for perfection each time you keep wicket.

7   **Kit**

- Acquire your own kit as soon as possible.
- Buy the best you can afford and aim for comfort above all else.
- For support and confidence wear compression shorts or Lycra swimming trunks.

8   **The Spirit of Wicketkeeping**

- If your skipper, coach or teammate gives you stick for walking, stay calm, look him in the eye, smile and say, "That's how I play".

9   Wicketkeeping and the Laws of Cricket

- Make sure you know the Laws of cricket so that you can appeal with confidence and debate with certainty.
- Volunteer to stand as umpire at every opportunity.

Endnotes

1   *Zen Bow, Zen Arrow*, John Stevens, Shambhala, Boston, 2007, p. 45.